Creative Training

of related interest

Staff Supervision in a Turbulent Environment
Managing Process and Task in Front-line Services
Lynette Hughes and Paul Pengelly
ISBN 1 85302 327 2

Good Practice in Supervision
Statutory and Voluntary Organisations
Edited by Jacki Pritchard
ISBN 1 85302 279 9

Focus on Psychodrama
The Therapeutic Aspects of Psychodrama
Peter Felix Kellermann
Foreword by Jonathan D Moreno
ISBN 1 85302 127 X

Dramatherapy
Clinical Studies
Edited by Steve Mitchell
ISBN 1 85302 304 3

Arts Approaches to Conflict
Edited by Marian Liebmann
ISBN 1 85302 293 4

Creative Training

Sociodrama and Team-building

Ron Wiener

Jessica Kingsley Publishers
London and Bristol, Pennsylvania

The right of Ron Wiener to be identified as author of this work has been asserted by him in accordance with the Copyright, Designs and Patents Act 1988.

First published in the United Kingdom in 1997 by
Jessica Kingsley Publishers Ltd
116 Pentonville Road
London N1 9JB, England
and
1900 Frost Road, Suite 101
Bristol, PA 19007, U S A

Copyright © 1997 Ron Wiener

Library of Congress Cataloging in Publication Data
Wiener, Ron.
Creative training/Ron Wiener.
p.   cm.
Includes bibliographical references and index.
ISBN 1-85302-422-8 (pb)
1. Employees - Training of. 2. Work groups. I. Title.
HF5549.5 T7W487 1997
658.3′124--dc20   96-31278
                                                        CIP

British Library Cataloguing in Publication Data
A CIP catalogue record for this book is available from the British Library

Printed and Bound in Great Britain by
Athenaeum Press, Gateshead, Tyne and Wear

Contents

To Ken, Ruth and Jennie
With thanks for their support and help to
Jaswant Bhavra, Doreen Dalgleish and Diane Jacks

Foreword

This book is written in three parts, each based on a manual originally published by the Department of Adult Continuing Education at the University of Leeds.

Each part stands on its own, though there is cross-referencing where appropriate. Some of the training techniques, such as sculpting, will therefore appear in all the sections, but their use will alter in each context.

Part One on 'Running Staff Training Groups' focuses on the way in which trainers can use action learning methods such as role play to put over their material.

Part Two on 'Team Doctoring' looks at how teams develop and then, in the second part, the strategies that a consultant can use to work with stuck or malfunctioning teams.

Part Three on 'Using Sociodrama' covers the use of sociodramatic techniques in training groups, as well as using sociodrama, a method in its own right, to explore group, social and political issues.

Throughout the book there is a concern that the trainer should be aware of issues to do with power and anti-discriminatory practice and the context within which training takes place.

Finally, while training is a serious matter both in terms of its professionalism and areas of concern, there should, where appropriate, be enjoyment as well. Humour gives energy and without energy nothing happens.

Ron Wiener

'We can't sedate
All the trainers
That we hate'

*Graffiti on a lavatory wall at a TEC
somewhere north of Watford.*

This book is written to remove the need for sedation.

'In the encounter lies the possibility of change.'

Ken Sprague 1996

Training which is passive, which provides no opportunity for engagement, is unlikely to produce any change beyond the workshop

PART I

Running Staff Training Groups

1. Introduction

1.1 INTRODUCTION

This section is aimed at members of training and/or human resource departments as well as those whose jobs involve some staff training. Its focus is on how to be a creative trainer rather than attempting to be a comprehensive guide to all aspects of training.

The second chapter covers the background to training – a look at how adults learn best, how trainees can be empowered and how any training session provides an opportunity for good practice.

The third chapter looks at who should do the training and how trainees can prepare for a session.

The fourth chapter examines how courses are set up and the planning that needs to go into them, while chapter five explores different ways of starting sessions.

The sixth chapter focuses on what goes on during a session and how a trainer deals with issues such as time, feedback and how to deal with bad practice.

Chapter seven looks at examples of the use of creative training techniques such as the use of role plays.

The final chapter considers what factors a trainer needs to take into account in ending a course.

1.2 THE TEAM LEARNING CULTURE

It is important to realise that the most useful training often takes place in the workplace rather than away on training courses. There are a number of reasons for this:

- o it is immediately relevant

- o it does not involve problems of transferring skills or knowledge from a training course back to the work setting o the process of training will have spin-off effects in terms of team building

o what is learnt is likely to be owned by the team and therefore space, time and support are more likely to be available for the learning to be implemented.

In any staff team there is a wealth of experience to draw on. If we assume, for example, that each member of a staff group has 50 dealings with members of the public a week, if there are 12 people in the staff team this means that there are a total of 600 dealings between staff and customers each week.

We can further assume that a third of their dealings will have been handled well, a third satisfactorily and a third, with hindsight, could have been dealt with better.

It is possible to learn from both ends of the scale, that is, to share the skills on the cases of good practice and to learn from an analysis of those which were not handled as well as they could have been.

For this learning to take place, a number of conditions need to be met:

o the staff group need to be working as a team

o the team needs a basis of good practice which can be built on

o there need to be existing team norms: to share, to encourage self-development and to expose individual practice to group scrutiny

o teams need to have people with group leading and facilitating skills

o teams need to have appropriate staff meetings.

A different way to approach the same issue is to ask how people in a staff team transfer skills between one another.

Sometimes, such as with the need to acquire new skills, team learning might not be sufficient and external courses are more relevant.

On other occasions the team might benefit from an external trainer when, for example, hidden agendas dominate team functioning and the informal rules that have been developed prevent anyone within the team from confronting the issue.

This section is intended to help both the team leader and the full-time trainer to run better sessions.

2. Background

2.1 INTRODUCTION

This chapter starts off by looking at the different ways in which people learn and then goes on to consider some pre-conditions for learning to take place and how secondary plots emerge.

2.2 WAYS OF LEARNING

Most people's experience of learning is that of the formal classroom setting of school and/or further education courses.

This is not a very appropriate model for adult learning because:

- o it denies the life and work experience that adults bring to the learning situation

- o it promotes the teacher/trainer as being the 'expert'. This:
  - de-skills the trainees by assuming the teacher has all the knowledge
  - assumes learning is a one-way process from teacher to student
  - makes it too easy to dismiss the content of the course by disqualifying the trainer. 'It's easy for her/him to do this here, but it wouldn't work in my crowded training centre.'

- o it is passive, seeing the student as a piece of blotting paper absorbing the teacher's wisdom. This is unrealistic because:
  - people's attention span is comparatively short
  - people only learn what they see as relevant
  - passivity takes away energy and energy is a necessary prerequisite of learning.

- o An ancient Chinese proverb sums up the best principles of training:
  - Tell me…I forget
  - Show me…I remember
  - Involve me…I understand

As we saw in the introduction, a typical staff team might well have a reservoir of thousands of incidents to draw upon. In this case the trainer's role becomes primarily that of a facilitator enabling participants to reflect upon the incidents, consider their implications and explore new ways of tackling them.

This is not to say that there are never situations where new knowledge has to be imparted, fresh skills introduced or standards set, but that the approach, even then, should embody the principles of adult learning discussed below.

There are six principles of adult learning (Brookfield 1986, p.72):

- o voluntary participation

- o mutual respect

- o collaboration

- o experience based

- o critical reflection

- o self-direction based on the individuality of each learner.

So how does the learning situation need to be structured? The most important aspects are that it must enable the participants' experiences to come to the fore in a way which they perceive to be relevant, and it must respect the different styles that participants might have.

One way of categorising learning styles identifies four types. There are accommodators, who learn from doing; divergers, who prefer concrete experience over abstract conceptualisation; convergers, who have a need to know how things work and learn by testing theories; and assimilators, who are logical and tend to form theories and seek facts.

Therefore the trainer needs a variety of ways of working to bring participants' experiences into the session and to meet the different learning styles. These might include:

- o brainstorming, where groups are asked to think as creatively as possible about an issue

- o project work such as setting team objectives

- o problem solving tasks

- o homework assignments

o role play.

One good rule for the trainer is to 'show, don't tell'. Therefore a group member in a discussion might recall a difficult incident with a client. The trainer, rather than asking him/her to talk the incident through, can, with the help of the group, enable the person to re-create the situation.

The advantages of doing this are that:

o it enables the group to see the scene rather than just hear about it

o it will carry more energy, which will engage the group at both an intellectual and emotional level

o the group can get involved in the interaction by making suggestions, taking on roles, exploring alternatives

o the individual, whose scene it is, can stand outside it and get a new perspective on it.

According to Burnard (1995, p.59), the basic principles of adult learning are that:

o there is an emphasis on action

o students are encouraged to reflect on their experience

o a clarifying approach is adopted by the facilitator

o there is an accent on personal experience

o human experience is valued as a source of learning.

These principles are important because, if the training session is to carry over into daily work, people must endorse its applicability – they need to own the learning. This is the difference between saying 'the trainer suggested a number of things we could do' and 'I now see that being more direct will improve my communication skills'.

2.3 EMPOWERMENT

Two further pre-conditions of effective learning are that people are able to learn and that they feel they are in a position to act on it. This needs to be tackled, in part, in the way that course members are selected, but it also needs to be a factor borne in mind by the trainer.

I was once asked to undertake some skills learning with a staff team. On arrival, it became clear that the staff had been going through a stressful period and felt totally dispirited. It was necessary to spend the first half of the day stroking, sometimes literally, the group before they felt in a position to tackle anything new.

Similarly, junior staff will sometimes feel that the training is irrelevant because they are not in a position to change anything. There are a number of ways of tackling this. Two of these are by getting people to:

o divide up situations into those they can change, those they might be able to change and those they cannot change and make sure the training covers the first two

o take on a more powerful role, such as a line manager or a trade union shop steward. This enables people to get an idea of what is possible and, even if they themselves do not have the power, whom they can influence to bring about change.

2.4 SECONDARY PLOTS

The need to empower trainees is only one example of secondary plots that emerge during the training process. While the primary focus might be skills learning, training opportunities often arise to team build, look at leadership styles or examine different ways of solving problems.

It is as if the agenda of a training session is a corridor with lots of rooms opening off it. Each of these doors leads into a room where a secondary training point could be made. For example, in a session on new legislation, someone might bring up a case to illustrate a point which also throws up the issue of how a client was counselled. If the trainer spends too much time in the room marked 'counselling', then there will not be enough time left to get to the end of the corridor. Sometimes it is sufficient to simply identify the door, by saying, 'This raises an important point about how we help clients, which, if we have time, we will consider later.'

In conclusion, the training manual is based on a theory that people learn best by doing. Subsequent chapters will look at how the trainer achieves this.

3. The Trainer(s)

3.1 INTRODUCTION

Trainers need:

- group work skills

- knowledge of their subject matter

- the ability to present material creatively

- the ability to create an atmosphere of support and trust

- a lot of energy

- time for preparation

- organisational skills.

Being a good manager or field worker, therefore, does not mean that someone will automatically be a competent trainer. As in many cases of promotion, trainers are sometimes selected on the basis of what they have done rather than on whether they have the skills to do the new job.

To put it differently, trainers need training, whether they are part of a training section or whether they are undertaking this function as a part of other duties.

It is also necessary to be clear which type of trainer can do what. Therefore team leaders are most appropriate when their teams are learning from their daily practice. Departmental training sections normally provide most basic training courses. External trainers or courses are needed to:

- cover any skills deficiencies in in-house training sections

- carry out team building where someone neutral in terms of institutional power and political position is essential

 o work with senior management where there is no one of
   sufficient seniority within the organisation.

In general, it is more cost effective to bring in a trainer rather than
to send people on courses. If it costs £75 a head to send a person on
a course, but the same trainer can be hired for £350 a day to run the
same course for 15 of the authority's staff, then the value for money
is clear. What is lost in this arrangement is the chance to exchange
experiences with staff from other agencies.

 One way of maximising an agency's return on an external trainer
is to have one of their staff participating as the junior trainer, picking
up the external person's knowledge and skills.

 This is one time when it makes sense to have two trainers. The
next section discusses the pros and cons of one or two trainers. The
final sections look at different ways a trainer needs to prepare
him/herself.

3.2 ALONE/IN PAIRS

There are many advantages to pairs working:

 o **Support.** Training is tiring physically and emotionally. A
   day's work is a little like a six-hour family therapy session.
   People need support before, during and after sessions. A
   person working alone needs to develop strong inner
   resources to be able to keep going.

 o **Supervisors.** All trainers need feedback on their work. This
   needs to happen beforehand in terms of planning sessions.
   It also needs to happen at breaks and after sessions, in
   evaluating what worked and what did not, what was going
   on in the group and devising new strategies.

Furthermore, because all training, whatever the content, has an
emotional level in which course members' feelings become projected into the group dynamics and onto the trainer as leader, the
trainer needs an additional system, perhaps from a partner or a
counsellor/therapist, in which she/he can work through their dealings with the emotional level of their work. This is important because trainers need to be aware of their own vulnerabilities.
Otherwise, they will steer the group away from areas they find
difficult or will get drawn into contentious issues without realising
it.

 o **Dividing up the work.** The trainer(s) has a number of roles
   to play, often simultaneously. These include course leader,
   recorder, administrator, the group's emotional maintainer,
   individual counsellor, information source, expert, advisor
   and facilitator. With two trainers, it becomes possible to

divide up the roles. For example, one trainer may take on the responsibility for course leader, facilitator and expert roles, leaving the other a secondary role in terms of direct input but having responsibility for observing what is going in the group, picking up individuals needs, giving support and supervision and fielding the inevitable knock on the door at a crucial point in the session.

The different roles can obviously be switched around between trainers during different parts of the course.

- o **Flexibility.** Working in twos enables a well-functioning pair of trainers to take risks. It becomes possible for one trainer, for example, to join in and give an input to a role play, while the other trainer then slips into the role of session leader and director.

There are, of course, disadvantages to pairs. These are:

- o The cost, perhaps financial but also in time: Trainers tend to be busy people and simply finding time for planning, running and evaluating sessions can be difficult.

- o Flexibility: The trainer is always faced with a number of paths which the group can travel to work its way through the sessions. There is a risk with working in pairs that, unless they are very empathic, the trainer leading the session will feel pressured to follow the pre-arranged path, which might not be the one which best meets the group's changing needs.

- o If trainers do not get on well with each other, or have different working styles, then there are likely to be tensions between them which will become disruptive, just as two adults with conflicting ways of handling children's behavioural problems will only make the problems worse.

3.3 WORKING TOGETHER

If two trainers are going to work together, then they need to spend time exploring each other's strengths and weaknesses, looking in particular at the possible areas of disagreement and considering how to tackle them.

One exercise which helps this process is for the trainers to take one pen, which they both hold, and draw on a sheet of paper, without talking, their own ideal house. The negotiations involved in doing this will give people a view as to how they might work together.

There are basically four different ways in which trainers can divide up sessions. They may:

o jointly run the sessions, interchanging the roles as necessary. This is only possible with two trainers who know each other very well and have compatible styles.

o divide up the different sessions, with one person taking the course leader role and the other the supporting roles and swapping these over from session to session. This works best with two trainers of equal seniority who do not have much experience of working together.

o divide up each session, with different trainers taking responsibility for fronting particular parts. This requires some trust so that change-overs can be flexible enough to take account of how the session is developing.

o have a senior and a junior. This happens where one trainer is more experienced and will perhaps take the main responsibility for running the course, with the junior one 'learning by sitting next to Nellie'. Obviously, it becomes possible to switch this responsibility over on a planned learning basis.

What is important is that, before training starts, the two people have considered fully the following: their individual power base, the power relationship between themselves and between them and the group, as well as core values such as how they will deal with feelings, their trigger points, attitudes towards anti-discriminatory practice, how they will handle difficult situations and a consideration of their own strengths and weaknesses.

3.4 'ISMS'

It is important, as a part of a trainer's preparation, that s/he is aware of how issues to do with gender, race, disability, age, sexual orientation, class, religion and culture might affect the course.

There are societal factors, in so far as existing differences in power in the wider society can be recreated in the course. This might well be reflected in the attitudes that participants hold towards each other – homophobic feelings being expressed, for example, during a discussion on sexuality.

There are structural aspects, such as the predominance of white male managers in the commissioning authority. This might well be reflected in what they want the training to cover or how employees are selected to participate. The training might, for example, be geared to full-time employees, while there could be a high percentage of female part-time workers who receive less than their fair share of training.

Similarly, middle management training might simply include existing people holding junior management positions, thereby reinforcing the existing racial bias.

There might well be institutional bias in a particular establishment. For example, newly trained professional staff will sometimes rubbish the learnt expertise of older workers who did not have their formal education opportunities.

The trainer needs, where possible, to be in a position to have a say in how these issues can be tackled when setting up his/her training programme.

This might be as basic as determining that there is wheelchair access and that a hearing loop, if required, is available.

The trainer also needs to be aware of how 'isms' might be showing themselves on his/her courses – for example, males dominating group conversations, outright racist remarks – and needs to have strategies for dealing with them.

Finally, the trainer needs to monitor continually what s/he says or does in terms of the effect it might have on people. Is s/he aware, for example, of treating men and women in the group differently?

3.5 OWN PREPARATION

As training is physically and mentally tiring, trainers need to make sure that they leave sufficient space to prepare adequately for sessions. This ranges from getting sufficient sleep, to leaving enough time in the diary for adequate preparation, to getting to the training location in sufficient time to make sure that the room is set up appropriately.

In conclusion, once trainers with the appropriate skills have been identified, the detailed planning of the training can begin and its implementation and evaluation arranged.

4. Planning

4.1 INTRODUCTION

The first task is to determine whether the call for training is meeting a real need. As will be discussed in other sections, people can ask for training for a number of reasons which have little to do with training needs.

One good example is child protection, where training might be carried out because central government money is available, because it is necessary for the authority to be seen to be doing something, or because it is cheaper than hiring new staff. Ideally, it would be in response to a researched need among particular groups of staff.

Again, training should reflect an organisation's aims and priorities. Otherwise, taking the case of child protection, how does one allocate resources between the competing needs of field, residential and survey staff and foster parents?

Training course objectives need to be worked out and set down in such a way that they can be measured and evaluated. Training courses can be evaluated in three ways. The first is at the end of the course. This measures the immediate impact. However, even if a trainer were to score 100 per cent on every dimension, this is not a very useful measure unless the learning is taken back into the workplace. Therefore, there needs to be a second evaluation a month later to see which aspects of the course are being utilised. The final evaluation needs to take place a further six weeks or so later to see if the use that the training has been put to has achieved any positive change in practice.

This chapter moves from discussing more general issues to the planning of individual sessions or courses.

4.2 LOCATING THE TRAINING WITHIN THE INSTITUTION

There are often a number of different explanations of how courses come to be put on:

o as part of a researched programme, based on individual training needs collated from different workplaces

o as a reflection of the needs or interests of the training department

o in response to national issues – the flavour of the year – (e.g. violence, sex abuse, disaster management etc.) This training comes about partly because of political commitment to good practices, for example 'equal opportunities', partly from pressure from field workers, partly because the institution, to protect itself, needs to show it is doing something in this area and partly because funds tend to follow flavours

o to meet a short-coming in the quality of an institution's service delivery. In recent years this has, for example, resulted in increased training for people in social service departments working in residential homes for young people.

Just as important in understanding why a particular training course is set up is identifying who, in the rest of the institution, is committed to its success.

A course on counselling skills might, for example, be set up because a training officer realises that it is a basic care skill that many staff are lacking. Responsibility for course recruitment might be left to joint line managers, who might nominate people for a variety of reasons.

The course will run, participants will gain an understanding of the fundamentals of counselling and go back to work and, if one is not careful, that will be it. In fact if some managers are not comfortable with counselling, they might actively prevent the embryonic skills being practised.

The course will only have been worthwhile if, in the sending of people on courses, arrangements have already been made to implement what the person will have been expected to have learnt. This might involve, for example, a staff team meeting to show other people what was learnt, or a supervisory system to monitor the skill development, or time and space arranged for the learning to be practised and possible senior management support to be given. In setting up a supervision training course for first line managers, it was also necessary to arrange a day for *their* managers, because it was unlikely that any supervision system they set up as a result of the course could be sustained unless they themselves received good supervision sessions.

Another time when senior management might need to be involved in order to make sure that course lessons are implemented is when junior staff are attending a course, because they will only have limited power to effect any change back at work. Again, the trainer needs to involve her/himself in all aspects of how the course is set up if it is to be as effective as it can be.

If the trainer is the staff team leader, then s/he must make sure that:

o the team as a whole sees the training as a priority and as relevant to its needs

o time and space have been set aside to take on board the lessons learnt from the training sessions

o there will be supervisory support and evaluation systems in place.

4.3 PARTICIPANTS

People come on to training courses for a number of reasons:

o They volunteer because they see it as relevant to their work – every trainer's dream.

o They are volunteered, or ordered to attend, because of agency policy or because it is seen to be in their interest – every trainer's nightmare.

o It is their turn in the office, even if the course is not particularly relevant.

o They are under stress and could do with a break. This is where training is seen as a holiday perk, especially if the venue is by the sea, has a swimming pool or is residential.

o Their line managers hope the trainers will be able to bring about an attitude change that they are reluctant to tackle.

o Management defines a problem as residing in a lack of individual skill rather than in institutional inadequacies. A workplace which has a number of troublesome incidents could analyse these in terms of poor leadership, lack of supervisory and other management systems or lack of skills of junior staff who, therefore, need training.

In general, blame is a power-laden concept; we tend to blame the people below us because it is better than analysing one's own defects. Therefore, we decide that it is the people below who need the training. This is the main reason why most training takes place at the level below where it is most needed. It is essential that a trainer has some idea of why people are coming to the session, because that will be a factor in determining how quickly the group is able to become an effective work group.

4.4 PLANNING THE SESSION

Sue Jennings (1986, p.10) suggests that there are four questions that need to be asked. These are:

- o What are my aims for the group?

- o What are the institution's aims for the group?

- o What are the group's aims for itself?

- o What are my aims for myself?

This suggests a way of proceeding which is to start with what the institution is asking the trainer to do with the group, such as 'better team functioning'.

It is then up to the trainer(s) to work out the ways in which this might be achieved, taking into account the interests, skills and needs of the group members.

Unless the topic is an entirely new area, it is important to remember that 80 per cent of the information will be known by the group. The trainer's job is to draw this out and help people reflect on it. There is no point in telling people what they already know. The trainer then has to find a way of feeding in the remaining 20 per cent. Of course the 80/20 split will be different for each course which, if forgotten, is one reason why running the same material for two separate groups might produce very different results – even if 'it worked last week!'

Finally, this provisional content needs to be checked out with the course members and adapted to take into account their demands.

Each particular part of the training day needs a framework. An example of one is given below:

Session:	1.30–4.30 p.m.
Subject:	Ways of restraining clients
Method:	Introductory talk / Warm-up game / Role play/ Discussions / Demonstrations/ Large group practice/ Small group work on guidelines
Objectives:	For course members to develop guidelines and learn basic techniques in restraining clients
Materials:	Flip charts/ Blu-tack/ Marker pens

Two further categories could have been **'Trainer'** (essential if the session was to be divided between two trainers) and **'Timings'**. As will be discussed later, training involves both chronological and energy time and too tight a timetable inhibits a trainer's flexibility in working with the group.

It might, for example, be that the role play can be adapted to incorporate the demonstration and that it makes more sense in terms of the session's unfolding logic for it to come there. What is important is that the objective is achieved; the method can and should remain flexible. It is as if planning a training course is like finding the buried treasure on the back page of a child's comic, where the reader is offered a variety of different paths to follow. The trainer, in her/his planning, starts off on one path. However, as the course develops, the group's interest and energy suggest that a different path would be better. What matters is that the treasure (the learning outcomes) is found and that the group has got there by using the paths which have maintained their active involvement.

There can sometimes be a problem in working with training packs, which often have quite a tight timetable. But a guiding principle in using packs is that trainers should feel free to adapt them or use parts of them selectively to match group interests and their own training styles. Unless the trainer feels compatible with the material s/he will not feel able to adapt it to the group.

When designing the content, trainers should keep in mind anti-discriminatory issues. This is to keep participants aware of how these issues can affect practice and also because it puts them in a context which can make them more relevant than if they are only discussed in the abstract at the beginning of a course.

4.5 EQUIPMENT AND AIDS

The basic tools of the trade are flip charts, pens and blu-tack. On top of this are audio-visual aids such as videos and overhead projectors. The main points are that:

o The trainer should feel comfortable with the equipment and should have checked it out before the session.

o It should not be used as an easy fill (e.g. 'I know, we'll show them that video on time management, they need to know about that.') It should tie in with the session's objectives.

o The equipment should service the session rather than have the training justifying the equipment. This happens sometimes when a training department invests heavily in some equipment, such as a video studio, and suddenly all training courses find themselves using video as a training tool.

Most equipment has limitations. Overheads, for example, are fine while they are projected but the information is lost as soon as the projector is turned off. Videos can be instructive but are one step removed; they are about someone else's situation, not about actual situations the group members have themselves experienced.

4.6 SIZE OF THE GROUP

The ideal size of a training group will reflect a number of different factors:

- content

- how it is to be tackled

- degree of commitment by course members

- amount of trust and safety required

- skill of the trainer.

The smaller the group the easier in general it is to maximise trust, but often it is difficult to generate a lot of energy. In a very large group there may be lots of potential energy, but there is the difficulty of steering it constructively while achieving sufficient safety in order to enable group members to take risks.

I often find that somewhere between 12 and 18 members works well for a facilitative approach, with a lot of emphasis on people 'doing'.

4.7 GROUP MEMBERSHIP

Does it make sense for everyone to come from the same establishment or from the same type of work, or is it better to mix them up? Again, is there ever a case for courses with only female or black members? The answers will depend on what the training is set up to achieve. If it is about team building, or learning from the team's experience, it will probably be better to use one staff team. If the training is looking at violence in social services, it makes sense for there to be staff from different types of establishments in order to build up an overall picture, to transfer skills and to realise how actions in one part of the service can cause problems for staff elsewhere.

If the training is concerned with assertiveness there is a case for having a course for women employees only, while one on 'challenging institutional racism' might find different advantages in having a course for both black and white people, and another for black people alone, exploring bases for action.

The same issues apply in terms of staff of different grades. An introductory course on management might well aim to have first line managers from different sectors together, while another on handling stress might gain from staff on different grades working together and gaining an understanding of the stress associated with different jobs.

4.8 NOTIFICATION

The trainer also has to write a programme for the course. This will tell people:

- o what the content and basic structure of the course will be, without giving too rigid a timetable. With a flexible timetable, the trainer is able to respond to the group's agendas

- o how the course will be run. If it is going to involve their active participation they need to know this. It is well to avoid the word 'role play', however, because many people have a block about it. 'Learning from experience' serves just as well

- o practical details (e.g. dates, starting and finishing times, exact address, car parking, refreshment arrangements).

4.9 WHERE?

In the case of staff training, the choice is whether to hold the training in the workplace or elsewhere. There are a number of different factors involved in reaching this decision:

- o the length of the session – if it is simply an hour and a half's team meeting given over to training, then, provided there is a suitable room, it will not normally be worthwhile moving to new premises

- o the availability of suitable premises within budget limits

- o getting away, which can help break the existing patters of behaviour and take people away from interruptions, although it does have the problem that lessons learnt have to survive the transition to the workplace.

- o whether or not relief is available. If sessions are taking place in a workplace, then it is important that someone answers the telephone and covers emergencies. This can sometimes be arranged on a swap basis with another team;

alternatively, half the team can attend the training one day and the rest on a second day

o whether or not the session is taking place in the usual workplace. If it is, this has the advantage of demonstrating how the team operates naturally – particularly useful for trainers involved in team building sessions.

4.10 SUITABLE PREMISES

Ideally, the session should take place in a large, comfortable room with soft, movable chairs, few desks, and usable wall space.

It is generally better to have sub-groups working in one large room than moving to and fro between a plenary room and meeting rooms. This is because:

o it makes observation difficult if people are scattered

o it wastes time if people are continually having to move and re-settle

o sub-groups work better if they are in eyesight of each other. They act as a disciplinary monitor of each other's performance. It also makes it easier for a single trainer to see which groups need support and to cope with groups who complete the task first.

In conclusion, the trainer needs to have thought about all aspects of the training before starting the course. This will be helped by envisaging each stage of the course as discussed in the following chapters.

5. Beginnings

5.1 INTRODUCTION

At the beginning, the trainer has to create the conditions which will subsequently enable learning to take place. In many ways the trainer is like a host at the beginning of a party. S/he has to welcome people, do the introductions, rescue the isolates, make sure everyone knows where things are and create the right atmosphere to ensure the party swings.

5.2 STARTING

The trainer, at the start of a group, has a number of different tasks. These are:

- o to create a group where people are not afraid to express what they really want

- o to find a common language

- o to handle the different agendas that people come with, which might include the formal agenda, people's past experience of training courses or of the trainer, their own work needs, personal fears, agendas imposed on them by their own staff team or their employing authority.

Trainers need to start off by introducing themselves and the course. They need to show themselves as warm, friendly, confident, knowledgeable, professional, good listeners and respectful of people's confidence. Trainees have done two things in attending the course: They have taken a day off work, and they have taken a personal risk in exposing themselves to a group. Therefore, the trainers need to show that their sacrifice of time will be worthwhile and that the course will be safe.

The next step is to have people sit in a large circle to introduce themselves, saying what brought them to the course and what will make it a good course for them. This serves a number of purposes:

o It establishes a ground rule that everyone speaks. Groups quickly establish informal rules and people will often have been on courses where some people speak a lot and some hardly at all. This might well reflect pre-existing class, race, sex or status differences or be established in the first sessions.

o It enables the trainers to hear the different agendas and to decide what they are going to do about them.

o It gives members an opportunity to express negative feelings about being there. There will be those who have been sent or only learnt about the course at the last minute and who will be angry. Often, simply being given the chance to say so and get it off their chest is sufficient.

o It serves as an entry to the course. People need to leave behind other concerns, whether back at work or at home, if they are to concentrate on the course.

o It acts as a group-building exercise with everyone sharing together.

o Finally, it lets the trainers learn something about the state of each of the group members.

The next stage is to sort out the house rules, everything from meal breaks to fire regulations.

After this comes the need to establish ground rules for the day. There is a problem here in that if this is done too early in the course, before the group has started to form, then many people will not feel confident enough to participate. On the other hand, if the trainer does not indicate his/her concern for issues such as anti-discriminatory practice, then this might make people from less powerful groups feel vulnerable.

One approach is to spend a little time on rules at the beginning but to come back to them later in the course. This helps to overcome the 'flight safety syndrome'. This is where, on a plane when the steward shows the safety procedure, most people stop listening. The same thing can happen on courses where people feel the trainer is going through the motions.

A good example would be the role of confidentiality. This needs to be established fairly early on. There are three basic rules:

o Nothing is confidential. Anything can be repeated outside the group.

o People can talk about what happened in the group, but only in a way whereby no individual can be identified.

o Everything is confidential and nothing about either process or content can be shared.

In my experience, the first is unsafe unless the session is simply to do with passing on information, while the third is too restrictive unless one is running a closed therapeutic group. In any other circumstances it is unlikely to be adhered to. Furthermore, if training is to be useful back at work, then there has to be some way to talk about what happened on the course.

There will also be a time later in the course when a participant starts to talk about something happening in their workplace. This is the time to repeat the discussion about confidentiality as people can now see its relevance.

Some of the rules, such as time-keeping, can often be sorted out at the very beginning. If the course is to start at 9.15 a.m. and, at that time, three or four course members are still missing, then the trainer can discuss with the members who are present whether they should start or wait. The arguments for starting are:

o it sets a bad precedent for the rest of the course if the starting time is not adhered to

o it is not fair to the people who have got there on time.

The arguments for hanging on for five to ten minutes are:

o it saves having to repeat oneself

o people might have legitimate reasons for being late, e.g. venue difficult to find, problems with parking, childcare arrangements etc.

o people arriving late might remain outsiders for the whole of the course

o it might be part of the culture of the profession/organisation for events not to start on time.

5.3 WARM-UP GAMES

Warm-up games are exercises that groups can do at different stages of training sessions.

In real life, we can spend two or three months running in a new staff team, building up trust and good working relationships. On a training course, this has to be done in two or three hours. Warm-up games are a way of speeding up this process.

Example 1. An introductory game.

Even after initial introductions, people are still unlikely to remember each other's name. A further game is to ask people to form a circle in alphabetical order of first names. This requires people to ask others what their name is – this both reinforces names and helps to build up interactions between course members. Once people are in a circle they go round, starting from the A's, calling out their name. Alternatively, the first person says my name is 'Assia'. The second person says this is 'Assia' and my name is 'Barbara'. The third 'this is Assia and Barbara and my name is Clyde'. This clearly reinforces everyone's name.

In general, warm-up games have a number of different functions:

○ They break down barriers. Often on courses there are people of different grades, which can create barriers; junior people feel intimidated by higher grades. Warm-up games bring everyone down to the lowest common denominator.

○ They build up group intimacy by involving people taking risks with one another.

○ They create energy. This is particularly important in the after-lunch session when people are often feeling like a nap.

○ They lead into the next session. For example, if one were running a session looking at the importance of touch in relation to ways of handling older people, then it would be useful to start with a warm-up game which involved people touching one another.

○ They can lower defences and open people's attitudes. The aim of training often involves getting course members to look at their work through new eyes. Warm-up games, by putting people into unusual situations, can help this to happen.

Example 2. Trust game.

This is best done with seven to ten people. Everyone stands in a circle and one person volunteers to go into the middle. The rest stand close enough to make sure that the person in the middle can't fall. The person in the middle, with their eyes shut, their feet together and legs stiff, then allow themselves to be pushed around the group or passed around the circle like a parcel. After a minute or two they stop, and someone else volunteers to take their place.

Trainer joining in?

The trainer joins in when:

- o it is important to show you are one of the group

- o it is important to lead from the front if, as in example 2, people in the group are hesitant

- o the group has been set up to do a difficult task such as in example 1, where each person has to remember all the other people's names in the circle. Here the trainer should go last as this is the most difficult position.

Trainers should not join in when there is any risk:

- o to group safety; for example, games which involve people getting into tight circles, when it is important for the trainer to stand outside and make sure that everyone is okay

- o that they might get emotionally involved and lose their objectivity.

When not to use warm-up exercises

There are a number of times when either warm-up exercises might be altogether inappropriate or a trainer should not use particular ones.

One example of when it would be inappropriate to use a specific game would be where it might clash with the cultural values of group members; or, for example, with a touch game, the need for a safe space would have to be considered.

A time not to use warm-up games at all might be in the initial stages of a group where people were giving very clear verbal and/or non-verbal messages that things like warm-up games were 'silly' or 'childish'. In this case the trainer would probably have to start with where the group was at and, if possible, open them up to accepting new ways of working.

Warm-up games can be used, then, at the beginning of courses, but they also have a role in the middle of courses, both to lead into sessions and also to keep the energy going. In addition they can be used just before the end of a course. After a long day, members are often feeling tired, and without a warm-up exercise there is little energy to finish the course well. The task might be as simple as the trainer saying: 'Walk around the room, reflecting on the course, and when you have worked out what you would like to say as a finishing statement, then find yourself a different seat.'

6. Middles

6.1 INTRODUCTION

When the session is up and running, the trainer needs to be continually aware of a number of things. These include the time when the group should break up; how to use the trainer's presence; what is going on in the group; how to deal with difficult incidents; and how to keep a record of the session. These are all discussed in this chapter.

6.2 TIME

There are two types of time that a trainer needs to be aware of: 'chronological' – the actual number of minutes – and 'energy' – the enthusiasm a group has for a task.

The same exercise, such as 'brainstorming', can last for 5 minutes with one training group while a second group might have sufficient ideas and still be sparking each other off after 20 minutes.

For the trainer, energy time is by far the most important because without energy there can be no learning. As mentioned elsewhere, the trainer is always faced with choices of which path to take a group on to best achieve the objectives. One good compass reference is to follow the energy.

A good measure of 'energy' is the noise within a group. This can be used to decide when to start finishing an exercise; the ideal time is just before the energy runs out. If this is done, then people will be left with a bit of unfinished interest in the topic, it is therefore available for discussion, either in a later session or in one of the breaks.

6.3 SMALL GROUPS

There are a great number of advantages in running much of the course in sub-groups of three to four members, provided the composition of the sub-group changes from session to session. The advantages are:

- o team building with everyone working with every other team member

- o group safety as cliques are broken down and people get to know each other

- o preventing a know-all or group bore from dominating the whole group

- o active group involvement. It is difficult to be a passenger in a group of three or four and, despite what people might say, course members in general appreciate being involved as this justifies their decision to come on the course.

Some points about working with small groups.

If setting different tasks for different groups, put people into sub-groups:

- o by asking them to form groups with people with whom they have not yet worked, or know least well

- o by numbering in a circle and then getting all the '1's to form one group, the '2's another and so on

- o by asking them to choose people who do not do the same type of work as themselves.

As can be seen, one primary aim is to get people to mix with each other.

Sub-groups do not all work at the same pace. Therefore it is important to have an additional task that the trainer can set the group which finishes first; otherwise, they will become bored. Once two sub-groups have finished, it is generally a signal that it is time for the exercise to finish.

Again, it is possible to use the interlinking concepts of chronological and energy time. The trainer can say 'five minutes to go', but the groups might run out of energy after two minutes, when the trainer can say 'time's up'. Alternatively, saying 'five minutes to go' might help groups to concentrate on the task and the energy might last for fifteen minutes.

If groups are stuck in completing a task, then one way of helping them is to get them to recall relevant specific incidents from their workplace that they can draw on.

6.4 FEEDBACK

Controlling feedback from sub-groups is one of the most difficult tasks a trainer has. In a typical case, for example, if each group has been asked to write down on pieces of paper ideas of what makes a good team, a group spokesperson will come to the front and pin up the group's efforts. S/he will then proceed to read out each of the ideas, checking back with her/his sub-group that s/he has got it right. This then happens with the next group.

This is a total waste of effort because

- Everyone can read the list, so there is not need for the spokesperson to read them out.

- The people in the spokesperson's sub-group know it anyway, so they tune off.

- The length of time the first spokesperson takes then becomes the norm for each of the other groups, because their content is just as important as the first group's.

There are a number of alternative ways of handling feedback, such as:

- The trainer pins up the lists, highlights any points s/he thinks are relevant and asks for any further ideas or comments (i.e. the group spokesperson is made redundant).

- Each sub-group's lists are passed around from group to group so everyone gets to see the others' work. This needs to have tight time limits but tends to keep most people involved.

- Have breaks during the exercise with one person in each sub-group remaining by their production to explain what they have done and the rest being free to wander around and see what the other groups are doing.

6.5 TRAINER RECORDING

When sub-groups are reporting back verbally or when there is a brainstorm session, the trainer needs to record key points. This shows the group that s/he recognises that what they are saying is important. This is especially crucial when a course has been set up on the premise that course members' experiences are important.

Furthermore, if good points are made and not recorded, then they will soon pass out of people's memories. This is one case where having two trainers can be an advantage as one can lead the session while the other acts as recorder.

Finally, the more salient a point is for a participant, the more faithfully must a trainer record it. Less important points can be paraphrased but to do that with ones perceived as being significant is to deny that significance for the individual.

6.6 RECORDING AND HANDOUTS

Use of A1 Sheets:

A1 flip charts are an essential tool. Because they are large:

- o they encourage sub-groups to think creatively

- o people will write in big enough print so that they can be pinned up as summaries of that group's thoughts.

An important point to remember is that if a group is nearing the end of a page it is necessary to give them another sheet; otherwise, the group stops working on the premise that there are only a couple of lines to fill. In other words, by the amount of paper a trainer gives a group, s/he is giving them a message as to the amount of work that s/he expects from them.

Use of walls:

Putting up completed A1 sheets on the wall serves a number of purposes:

- o it helps the group to identify with and own the room

- o it takes away the need for individuals to be taking notes all the time

- o it gives feedback to the group as to how hard they have worked

- o it enables the trainer to refer back easily to earlier stages of the course

- o perhaps most importantly, it provides the basis for the group to make their own course handouts in the final session. On many courses, trainers give handouts which, if not seen as immediately relevant, will be put into the course folder, transferred into the training file at work and never read again. If the participants make their own course report, it will be both owned and contain within it those aspects of the course that the trainees see as relevant for them.

An example of this was at a course on chairing meetings, where participants designed their own self-evaluation checklist for examining how well they had carried out the tasks of a chairperson after each meeting.

6.7 PROCESS AND CONTENT

The trainer needs to keep aware of both what the group is working on and how it is working on it.

The question the trainer should be continually asking is: 'What is going on in this group and how can I use it?'

The trainer needs to keep in mind the different stages of a group's development – forming, storming, norming and performing – as this will help her/him to understand what is happening.

A lot of chatter might be an indication that this is an issue that a lot of people have something to say on, and it therefore makes sense to break down into small groups to allow this to happen.

Alternatively, if there is a lot of irrelevant chatter, it might be a sign that this part of the course is not meeting people's needs and that the trainer should re-negotiate the agenda with them.

In general, the trainer needs to be listening all the time to what is happening, and working out the best way to proceed. This will involve: summarising, negotiating, listening, using humour and a whole variety of other skills.

The best path is the one that enables course members to draw upon their experiences and use them in a way in which something new will have been learnt which is in keeping with the objectives.

6.8 BAD PRACTICE

Sometimes on training courses people either recount an incident or show, during discussion or role play, examples of bad practice. These can range from racist comments, to someone from a children's home boasting that he was known as 'Hitler' because of the physical manner in which he sorted out scraps between the children. Then too there are examples of insensitive handling of customers, and managers failing to pay any attention to staff's or clients' interests in determining policy.

In working out how to respond to these incidents, the trainer needs to be clear about:

- her/his authority. As an external trainer s/he often has no line management responsibility for people on the course, though this will be different where team leaders are running sessions for their own team

- the authority's policy on issues like equal opportunities, sexual harassment and dealing with violence

- her/his own values and when it is appropriate for these to be made clear.

There will, therefore, be a number of options the trainer can take. The trainer may:

- report back to senior management with appropriate line management responsibilities, or to the people who commissioned the training. Here the question of course confidentiality has to be balanced against collusion and the need to protect people

o challenge. While this, on some occasion, might be appropriate (for example, so that a racist remark is not condoned), there will be other times when a challenge or confrontation will simply result in defences going up and no behavioural change taking place

o suggest an alternative. The trainer can say 'have you thought of tackling it like this?' and can model the appropriate behaviour. Or the trainer can ask the group for suggestions

o role play. This can sometimes by reinforced by role playing the bad practice and an alternative scenario where the interaction is handled well, and letting the person either experience what it is like to be on the receiving end or hear what it is like from the person playing the role.

6.9 CHALLENGES TO THE TRAINER

'This course is no good'; 'None of this is relevant'; a person reading a paper during a session; people arriving late etc. How can the trainer handle situations like this?

o The trainer can listen, accepting that what is said might be true and offering to re-negotiate the agenda. S/he can also listen to hear whether there are reasons behind the statements, such as 'basically we are powerless junior staff working in an unprofessional situation and this training is just an attempt to buy us off', and then work with the group on these feelings and the realities underpinning them

o The trainer can reflect the problem back to the group – 'do you all feel like this?' or 'how do you handle differences in your own work team?'

o The trainer can admit that s/he is not God and is not all knowledgeable and use the collective group skills to find a way of dealing with the situation.

o S/he can spend time with disaffected individuals in breaks, trying to find out what is going on for them and how their needs can be met

o S/he can ignore the behaviour unless it is disruptive to the group. There is always the risk that picking up on an individual's behaviour might take attention away from the group's needs as a whole o S/he can look at what it is that the trainer might be contributing. Is there something in an individual trainee's attitude which triggers something in the trainer? Were the instructions unclear? Is the group safe enough for the tasks they have been asked to do?

Just as a good staff team is one without hidden agendas, the same applies to training groups. If necessary, the trainer needs to stop, reflect back to the group what s/he feels is going on, listen to their feelings and find some way of negotiating a way forward.

The trainer is providing a model for course members of how to tackle such issues – another example of a secondary plot.

6.10 TRAINER'S PRESENCE

Trainers can use their bodies to give messages to the group by:

o where they stand – usually in the centre of the group if the trainer is acting as course leader, or where they can be seen equally by all if acting as the facilitator. It is also possible to give support by standing near a person

o how they stand – for example, there are different messages that are given if the trainer joins a sitting sub-group from a standing position (checking up; supervision), by crouching (on same level; offering help if required) or by pulling up a chair (I am joining your group).

o how they move in relation to what they say – for example, if the trainer asks the group to stand, it is important that s/he stands too.

Everything the trainers do, therefore, is giving the group a message – how they move, how they hold themselves, the tone of their voice, how they handle disruptions and so on.

In summary, then, it is necessary for a trainer to be continuously aware of the interaction between meeting the session's aims, how the group is organising itself to do this and what the trainer's choices are.

7. Creative Training Techniques

7.1 INTRODUCTION

This chapter will look at ways of delivering training material creatively and, in particular, at the use of sculpting and role play.

If the delivery of the content is not made interesting, then the message will be lost. Take, for example, the issue of confidentiality. It is possible to give a talk about it. Alternatively, the trainer could ask people in the group to swap handbags and/or wallets. S/he then says, 'Without actually doing it, how would you feel if I now asked you to look through the bag you have?' People generally say they would not want to do it. People are now engaged with the topic and it becomes possible for the trainer, perhaps via small group discussion, to explore who has what right to know what about whom. In many public sector organisations, for example, personal information about service users is held by a number of different people – what are/should be the rules about this?

7.2 FACTUAL

Giving people a lot of information to digest rarely works because:

- o there is a limit to what people can retain

- o people only have a short-term attention span

- o most lecturers' delivery fails to hold people's interest.

It often works better if the trainer recognises that the aim of the session is to make participants see the purpose and relevance of the information, which can then be given as a handout. This can be done with new legislation, for example, by setting up a role play scene which shows what happened pre-legislation, then repeating the scene showing where, at key points, because of legislation, different practices are necessary. An example of this approach would be where, working with the police, a shop scene was created and shoplifting situations were set up so the group could discuss what offence was being committed when, according to which piece of legislation.

Other ways of putting information over include:

o a pub quiz format with group members in competing teams

o using drawing. In child protection work the trainer can get group members to draw, on the outlines of children's bodies, examples of evidence of different kinds of physical abuse. Or, when looking to make a workplace safe, the trainer could ask people to draw areas of potential danger on a floorplan of their work situation

o using what is around. In health and safety training, people could be sent around the area in pairs to record everything they think might be a hazard

o making it a game. In teaching building society employees about calculations to do with mortgage payments, the trainers devised an adapted game of monopoly

o using visualisation. It often helps if people can see a problem. For example, the trainer says, 'Show me what the health service looks like at the moment.' The group in question used their bodies to create a creaking machine running short of fuel. This can then be used as a starting point to begin talking about changes in the NHS. This is an example of sculpting, which is described next.

7.3 SCULPTING

In sculpting, objects or people are used to depict a set of relationships. Thus, if one was wanting to show the relationship between a boss and a worker, this might be shown in a stereotypical way, as the boss standing on a chair, pointing a finger at a worker who is sitting on another chair, cowering. This would make clear the perceived power differences between the two via the height and the body positions. People could then explore, by changing the sculpt, how this might be different if:

o the boss adopted an alternative management style

o the worker had an independent power base; for example, s/he was also a shop steward

o one or both of the actors were female or black or older persons.

In a sculpt, therefore, how and where people stand is important. For example, people back to back might indicate a lack of communication. If this were shown by people looking at how a multi-disciplinary team worked, it would then be possible to see whether this was due to personal, professional or organisational factors.

Equally important is the body position people take. This would be relevant in exploring in assertion training what body position conveyed an assertive message, as opposed to a submissive or an aggressive one.

Similarly, in work with violence and aggression, sculpting can be used to show the effect on a staff team dealing with a very challenging resident and also to model ways of working, such as adopting a relaxed stance.

Sculpting can be used in other ways to show the structure of an organisation, its usefulness in induction sessions, or to reveal the wider working environment of a team or department within an organisation.

These sculpts are static. They are therefore often a very safe way of getting course members to work experientially as they do not need to move or to say anything as they would have to in a role play.

An expanded version is where sculpting is used to follow the path of a case or process. This might, for example, involve tracking what happens in a child protection case from disclosure to a teacher, to designated teacher, social worker, through strategy meetings to the case conference; or it might follow what happens to a sample in a hospital pathology laboratory. Here, each person takes on the role of one of the characters/stages in the process. Again, there is no need for them to move or necessarily speak. Although the trainer can describe what is happening at each stage, this denies the existence of group knowledge. What works best is allowing each person to describe what they do and how they make decisions as to where 'it' (the case or sample) goes next. If at any stage someone holding the role is not conversant with the procedure, the trainer protects them by making it a group question – 'Who knows what happens here?'

This flow can be aided by different coloured balls of string which might reflect, for example, whether any intervention is advisory or carries accountability.

If the group is willing, then small role plays can be added in, so the group can hear, as an illustration, the phone call between the designated teacher and the social worker.

This type of sculpting is useful in a multi-disciplinary context to show people what goes on behind closed doors in the other organisations which affect their contribution. It is also valuable in helping people understand a process and thereby identify how it might be re-engineered.

7.4 ROLE PLAY

Role play can be used to:

- o learn from incidents by enacting them. It enables the group to explore questions such as 'what else could have been done?' and 'what techniques would have been useful?'

- o develop skills in, for example, counselling or assertion training sessions by setting up scenes which approximate real-life settings.

Role plays have the advantage of:

- o being able to use people's own experiences and therefore giving them a chance to reflect on and learn from them

- o being able to practise skills safely

- o letting people see the world from others' viewpoints by taking on different roles.

Role plays often have a bad name and promote anxiety when suggested on courses. This is because:

- o If the group does not feel safe, then it is threatening to be asked to display one's level of professional competence in front of one's peers

- o Some professionals, such as fieldworkers in social service, health and probation departments, nearly always work on their own and are therefore totally unused to their work being on display. It is possible, in fact, to be a fieldworker and for no-one to have ever seen you in action with a client for the whole of your working life

- o A lot of people have experienced badly-run role play sessions.

Before starting, it is necessary to have spent time making the group safe and warming people up. Role plays cannot work successfully until the group has jelled. Warm-up games can be useful here.

Because of the anxieties around, it is often better to slide into the role play rather than making a big pronouncement about it. It is also important to give people the opportunity to take a more passive function initially, for example, as an observer.

As an example, let us assume we are dealing with interviewing techniques. There are a number of ways we could proceed:

- o start with a sculpt of interviewer and interviewee and then add words

- o divide the group into pairs and ask each pair to devise a role play which they will then show to the group

- o set up a role play using the whole group.

In all cases there are a number of points the trainer has to keep in mind. They are:

- o clarity about the learning points. A role play, unless tightly scripted, will develop a life of its own, and the learning points become the places where the trainer needs to halt the action

- o the pace of the action. Stopping the role play too frequently means it becomes disjointed; not halting it often enough means learning points are lost

- o everyone needs a role. Even if there are only two people performing, the rest need to be given specific tasks as observers, for example, 'I would like you two to look for examples of appropriate non-verbal behaviour.' This is because, without a focus, people do not know what to look for and it becomes a play rather than a learning situation

- o the need to protect the role players so that people do not come out of the situation feeling worse than when they went in. One necessary task, as we have said, is to make sure that the group feels safe and has moved beyond the storming stage.

The persons who are most at risk are normally those who have to show their professional skills in front of their peers. In this example it would be the person playing the interviewer. The risk to others comes primarily from being emotionally triggered. In any group of ten people, the chances are that there will be one or two who have suffered from sexual, physical or emotional abuse as children and the trainer needs to be aware that emotional scenes might produce a reaction. This is one of the reasons why de-roling at the end of a session needs to take place.

There are a variety of ways that people can be protected. These include:

- o people not playing their normal role, for example, managers playing junior staff

- o people being asked initially to play a role badly. This has a number of advantages. It is usually humorous (this is the format used in many of the Cleese training films); there is a lot of learning on how not to do it and, finally, when asked to do it well, people will be confident that they can improve on their first effort

- o people playing a group script. Here, whenever someone looks like getting stuck, the trainer stops the action and asks the group what they think the interviewer should say or do next. The 'interviewer' can then choose one of the group suggestions and, if it does not work, then this is due to the suggestion not being appropriate rather than the role player not getting it right

- o the role players being given a tight script by the trainer so they are simply reproducing someone else's lines

- o in times of difficulty, people being asked to reverse or swap roles. For example, if the interviewee asks 'what gives you the right to ask me that question?' and it looks like the interviewer is struggling to find an answer, the trainer can swap them over so that the interviewee becomes the interviewer and answers her/his own question. This is also very useful in helping people see the situation from an alternative perspective. It is also possible to reverse roles with someone who is an observer – 'Why don't you have a go at being the interviewer?'

- o people in a role being given a double (or support) person. In this case, this would be someone sitting next to the interviewer, who could be a silent support, someone who chips in and makes suggestions if it looks like the interviewer is stuck, or someone who voices the unexpressed thoughts or feelings the interviewer might have

- o the trainer giving support by her/his presence.

Keeping the above in mind, let us assume that we want to run the role play in front of the whole group. The first task is to devise a scene. It can be either pre-scripted by the trainer, or the group can be allowed to create the script. The advantage of the former option is that the trainer can ensure the script matches his/her learning points. The disadvantage is that there is no guarantee that it will grab people. In general, it is better to allow people to build up a script: 'Who is the interviewer? How old? What gender/role?' 'What is the interview about?' This involves the group and allows them to contribute the energy they will retain from similar situations they have been in.

The next stage is how to choose the people to fill the roles. If the trainer simply says 'Who would like to be the interviewer?', s/he is likely to find that everyone develops a sudden interest in the floor or the ceiling! What tends to work best is for the trainer to choose the first person and then adopt serial choice. The first person will have carried bonus points by having saved everyone else in the group. The trainer can cash these in by asking the first chosen to pick the next player and so on down the line.

Re-enacting

A different type of role play is where participants are re-enacting a scene. This might be in assertion training, where a person wants to review how they handled a scene.

In this case the trainer helps the person or protagonist to re-create the scene. A useful way of starting is to construct the physical environment where the scene occurred. This helps to warm up the person to the exercise.

The next task is to show what the scene was like. To do this we have to get to know what the other actor(s) in the scene were like. One way of doing this is to let the person whose scene it is swap roles and show the rest of the audience what they were like and how they acted. This then cues the person who is to take this role as to what they were like and how to play it.

Once a role starts, it does not have to follow exactly what happened for it to be a useful learning exercise. There is nothing worse than the person stopping the exercise to say 'he didn't use those words'. This both stops the actors developing their roles and takes energy away.

What is important, however, is that the protagonist has a chance at the end to say exactly what did happen, because for him/her the session will always be in part a therapeutic re-living of the original.

Often it is a good idea for the protagonist not to play her/himself. This is because:

o S/he might get bogged down in the need for historical exactitude.

o S/he might learn more from playing another role or standing outside it altogether as an observer.

o Often a scene a protagonist will choose to re-enact will be one where the other person was either very difficult or aggressive. If the role play is to be effective the energy that goes with this role must be re-captured. One way of doing this is to get the protagonist to take on the role of the other.

The action can then develop using role reversal, doubles and appropriate pauses to explore the issue.

Forum role play

A different way of progressing a role play is to adopt Boal's (1992) work on forum theatre. This is particularly appropriate where aggression is involved. Therefore, if we take the assertion example, where a person feels s/he handled a scene badly, in forum role play the scene would be played through first exactly as it happened.

The scene would then be repeated, but each time one of the rest of the group saw a way that the person could have done or said something different, they would shout 'Stop'. The trainer would then invite them to come up and take over the protagonist role and show their version of how it could be handled. The trainer would then stop it, let the learning be drawn especially in terms of how the other person reacted to this intervention. The trainer would then get the original person to pick up the scene again, at the point where it was interrupted, until someone else shouted 'Stop'. This was used very effectively in a Boal Workshop in order to explore options open for a person in a wheelchair who was refused access to a shopping centre.

Because there is immediate feedback, this is a good way to try out ways to confront oppression. It does, however, require a safe working group environment in order for people to volunteer their options.

Using video

Videos are a good way of initiating a role play. Videos on their own – for example, on a counselling session – are useful as a way of reflecting on the skills on display, but they still remain one step removed from group members owning them. Therefore, a video can be paused and group members can be given the roles of the actors on the video and asked to take the scene on, using the skills they have just been observing.

Particularly in skills development, videoing role plays is a way in which participants can review and reflect on their performance. This also gives scope for the different learning styles that participants might have. If cameras are not available, the same effect can be achieved by using the group to give feedback, either collectively or with people working in small groups, with one or two people being given specific observer roles.

The trainer as director

With all of this going on, it is important that the trainer acts as the scene's director, keeping everything under control and safe. This might, for example, involve right at the beginning setting down the rules for physical contact if the scene is likely to contain any aggression.

The trainer needs to be very careful, therefore, before getting involved in any way in the action, because, once involved, there is no one left in control and the situation might well feel unsafe.

Confidentiality

One issue which always crops up in re-running incidents is whether real names should be used. Sometimes participants have strong feelings against doing so, which need to be respected, but otherwise I prefer to re-establish a rule about confidentiality and use real names. This is because once the action begins, the real names often slip out, and because it makes it easier for the protagonist to recall the scene.

De-roling

It is essential to take people out of their roles at the end of session. A trainer is a bit like Moses – wherever s/he takes people to, s/he has a responsibility to bring them back. As a start, people should always be moved physically from where they were playing a role. Then one way of de-roling is to get people who have been in role to turn to someone else and mention three ways they were not like the character they played and one thing they like about themselves or re-count one good bit of work they have done recently.

It is still necessary for the trainer to check for her/himself that this has worked for all people.

Sharing

It is usually useful for the actors to have the opportunity to share about how it felt in role before they de-role.

It is always a good idea to give everyone, at the end of the session, an opportunity to share with the group any feelings or thoughts they have about the role play. This is because:

o it might have stirred up painful memories for other people of similar incidents they have been involved in

o it lets the protagonist know that other people have faced similar incidents and felt like s/he did

o it provides an opportunity for reflection and learning.

Conclusion

Role play can be a very powerful tool to practise and explore what might happen in a planned work session. It is very useful for staff groups either as a means of analysing what went wrong or sharing a skill.

In one adult training centre, staff replayed incidents with a trainee to look at what might be provoking her tantrums. After seven re-runs, they isolated the colour yellow as being the trigger, and what had appeared random acts became predictable and controllable.

For trainers, role play is a method of bringing into a course participants' experiences so that they can become part of the course's learning material.

8. Endings

8.1 INTRODUCTION

There are two entirely different ending tasks for the trainer. The first concerns the content of the course – what has been learnt and how it will be implemented. The second is to do with participants sharing how they have been feeling in the group together and giving each other feedback.

8.2 COURSE CONTENT

It is no use for someone to come back to work from a course saying 'That was an interesting three days.' People cannot act on a generalisation. It is much more beneficial for a person to report back, 'What I learnt was the need for us to have a weekly team meeting and structured fortnightly supervision sessions.'

Therefore, in the last session it is important to get participants to write down specific, actionable things they have got from the course. One way of doing this is as follows:

- o Give each participant 15 minutes to write down 5–15 things from the wall charts that they have learnt from the course.

- o Then move into pairs, share lists and come up with the five most important points.

- o Finally, each pair calls out their points, which the trainer writes up.

The next problem is to get the points implemented back at work. This is where the importance of how people were selected becomes apparent. If they are very low in the hierarchy, then it becomes difficult for them to make suggestions which would involve institutional change. It is also worth remembering that institutions are better prepared to resist change than to embrace it. This is where the failure to contract properly with line managers creates difficulties.

Therefore, it is important at this stage for the trainer to raise the question of what will stop any learning being acted on. Here, it makes sense for participants to work in small groups with those who can, post-course, give them most support. It might be people from the same workplace, from the same grade or who do similar work. The sub-groups might be asked to look at what will make change difficult and to work out strategies for tackling the difficulties. The trainer can move around acting as a consultant to each of the groups.

A further stage or a different set of questions is to ask people in workplace groups what will have changed in one and in three months' time as a result of having been on the course. Again, it is worth asking the groups to examine the process of how these changes will come about.

Very often the trainer will find that there will not even be a staff meeting with time set aside for people to feed back on training events they have attended, which is a sign of poor course planning.

Useful suggestions the trainer can make include:

- looking for allies among the staff group or from staff involved in similar work situations

- rehearsing what needs to be said with the participant's supervisor

- exploring the areas where the worker has some control over her/his functioning.

It is sometimes useful for participants to make public the changes they intend to bring about, as this is likely to make them take them seriously. This is particularly so where there is going to be a follow-up session.

Follow-up sessions have a number of uses. They:

- provide the opportunity for support

- enable the lessons from the training session to be reinforced

- increase the likelihood of course learning being implemented, especially if projects are set at the end of training day(s)

- give participants the opportunity to refine their implementation strategies.

8.3 PARTICIPANTS SHARING

People on a training course have spent time together as a group with varying degrees of trust, intimacy and sharing. People need some time to say goodbye to each other in a way that enables the interactions and feelings generated during the day/s to be satisfactorily released.

In addition, people will have opened themselves to others and the course, therefore, provides them with an opportunity to receive feedback on how they come across. More importantly, it gives people the space to practise giving and receiving positive feedback on work performance.

If I ask people on a course 'When was the last time that someone told you that you had done a good piece of work?', the majority will be hard pressed to give an answer.

Giving and receiving compliments is not something that most people find easy to do. We are more likely to be suspicious of a compliment, wondering perhaps what the person was after. Whether badly or sincerely done, a compliment can quite easily come over as patronising, so practice is useful.

One way of doing this is to get the participants to stand and go round everyone else in the group and give each person some feedback on what they have learnt about them. The number of minutes allowed for this task should be double the number of people in the group.

This also provides space for the trainer to give her/his own comments to each participant. This feedback can become powerful as a result of the expertise and skill that the group members perceive as characteristics of the trainers. This is particularly so in the case of well-run courses.

A similar way of doing this exercise is for everyone to have a piece of A4 paper sellotaped to their back. Armed with a pen, everyone writes something on everyone else's back.

An alternative way is for each person to blu-tack an A1 sheet to the wall at lunchtime on the last afternoon. Again, people are expected during the final sessions to find time to write something on each person's sheet.

The main advantage of the last two methods is that people have a sheet of paper, often with a series of positive comments to take away with them. The drawbacks are that, unlike the first, it takes away the need to handle compliments face to face and makes it difficult for people to explore with the writer any questionable comments.

Moving on to saying goodbyes, one way of doing this is to get everyone to form a circle and to say, in turn, something which summarises the training session for them. This makes sure that no-one is left out and it also provides an opportunity for people to let go of feelings.

It does two further things in addition: First it provides some instant evaluation of the course. This is necessary both for the body organising the training session and also for the trainer. An additional method for getting evaluation is for a short questionnaire to be handed out and either filled in on the spot or posted back later. If the latter is done, the response level drops off sharply. If the former, people have to be assured of confidentiality if the responses are to be honest.

Second, it gives the trainer feedback on her/his performance. The better the performance, the harder the work, the more the trainer has earned her/his applause. It is no different from the end of a stage play with the actors receiving some emotional input to balance what they have given out.

While in the sitting circle, sharing is primarily an individual's response to the course, but people also need to have the opportunity to share their feelings to the group as a whole. One way of doing this is to ask people to stand with their arms around each other (assuming that is in keeping with how course members feel towards each other) and for them to say anything they want to the group as a whole.

8.4 THE GROUP PROCESS

Another bit of learning that can sometimes be included in the final session is giving participants the opportunity to reflect on how the training group has (or has not) worked. During the session there will have been some team building, a variety of group processes, one or more leadership styles shown by the trainer/s and an illustration of how to run training courses.

This can be done either by brainstorming or by dividing up into subgroups.

8.5 THE TRAINER'S NEEDS

The trainer needs:

- ○ feedback on her/his performance. This can come from a co-trainer, a supervisor, an observer, course participants and self-evaluation

- ○ support. This requires a sympathetic ear from family, friends, therapist and other trainers

- ○ a chance to wind down. This can be via support and/or sport, sleep, drink etc.

A trainer is as likely to suffer from burn-out as any worker and s/he must make sure that the session is processed and space created for the next piece of work.

REFERENCES

Boal, A. (1992) *Games for Actors and Non-Actors*. London: Routledge.

Brookfield, S. (1986) *Understanding and Facilitating Adult Learning*. Buckingham: Open University Press.

Burnard, P. (1995) *Learning Human Skills*, 3rd ed. London: Butterworth-Heinemann Ltd.

Jennings, S. (1986) *Creative Drama in Groupwork*. Oxon: Winslow Press.

PART II

Team Building and the Art of Team Doctoring

1. Introduction

1.1 AIMS

The aims of this part are to provide a framework and a manual for people working in and with staff teams to understand and improve their functioning.

1.2 STRUCTURE

This part is written in two sections. Section I looks at the different stages a team passes through and the role of the team doctor at each stage. Section II looks at the different techniques available to the consultant or team doctor and how they can be used.

2. SECTION I
Stages of Team Development

2.1 OUTLINE OF SECTION I

Section I looks at seven stages of human development, described in a stereotypic way, as an analogy for team development. These stages are as follows:

1. Conception and Pregnancy

2. Birth

3. Infancy

4. Adolescence

5. Maturity

6. Middle Age

7. Senility

Each stage is analysed from three perspectives:

(i) Team tasks

(ii) Senior management responsibilities

(iii) Role of the team doctor

2.2 FIRST STAGE: CONCEPTION AND PREGNANCY

2.2 (i) Team Tasks

At some stage, the need for a new staff team becomes apparent. It might be due to the setting up of a day centre, a project team, a hospital ward or a new workplace, or as a result of a departmental re-organisation.

Right from the beginning there needs to be some thinking about the membership of the new staff team. This will be dependent on the aim of the team, the underlying philosophy, the method of service delivery, the type of client/customer and the range of skills needed.

The ability to select staff will be affected by resource limitations, local and national wage and employment agreements, availability of staff, comparison with working conditions in surrounding areas, the advertising of openings, equal opportunity policies and selection procedures.

Staff need to be in post when the place opens. But before the birth, other things need to happen. The first of these is the selection of a good team leader. It cannot be emphasised strongly enough that this is the single most important step in establishing an effective staff team.

Some of the general attributes that good leaders should have are: to be able to get the best from people; to be comfortable with people; to be a good listener; to be available; to be a simplifier; to be fair; to be persistent; to be decisive; to trust; to be a good delegator; to do the dogsbody work when necessary; to give honest feedback; to have respect for people; to know the business; to be open; to keep promises; to admit personal mistakes; to listen; to teach; to facilitate; to give space; to take blame when appropriate; to give credit where due and to have a preference for face to face intervention rather than memos (Peters and Austin 1986, p.355).

In addition to the general attributes, the team leader will need to have specific skills and knowledge in relation to the team task. This doesn't necessarily mean that the team manager has to be the most skilled person, but s/he has to know enough to have credibility, recognise quality and, more importantly, to have the ability to utilise all the team's strengths.

Once the team leader is chosen s/he will need to be involved in the selection of the rest of the staff. A number of different criteria will need to be kept in mind in choosing staff. These include:

o the skills, attitudes and experiences of applicants and how these match with the demands of the team's work

o how team members are likely to get on with each other. Though all team members need to get on with each other if the benefits of working in a team are to be realised, some teams – for example, those working in a therapeutic community – will require much greater levels of intimacy and trust o that team task roles are balanced out. All teams, if they are to be productive, require a number of different roles to be filled. Whichever classification of roles is used (see Belbin 1981 for an example), teams need someone to: have ideas; see they are taken up; research and question their implications; get them put into action; coordinate and oversee the enterprise; see that the action doesn't fizzle out and check how it is going and whether it was worth doing in the first place. Unfortunately, in many staff teams, all the 'someones' end up being the same person, the team leader. One consequence of staff teams like this is a series of half-finished projects resulting in a general feeling of dissatisfaction

o organisational policies such as those relating to equal opportunities.

2.2 (ii) Senior management responsibilities

The senior manager/s are responsible for:

o the selection of the team leader

o setting out the team's initial aims

o allocating resources – physical and financial – so that the team can start operating

o being clear as to how the team will fit into the rest of the organisational structure

o determining what type/system of information technology is most appropriate for the team's needs

o working with the team leader to develop an initial business plan.

2.2 (iii) Role of the team doctor

The role of an outside consultant is usually limited to helping out with the recruitment and selection of key staff.

If one pays a staff member £20,000 with annual staff support overheads of £2,000 per annum, and if each person remains on average for five years, then each selection is an investment of at least £110,000. Yet I still know of employers where seven minutes is seen as a long time to allocate for a selection interview.

Increasingly, therefore, consultants are being used to make sure that the investment pays off. Sometimes the consultancy will be used to run selection interviewing courses for staff, sometimes to run psychometric tests, sometimes as an outsider giving independent advice and sometimes by providing a total interview package.

The consultant's aim is to see how people function in the environment they are coming into. Applicants are therefore often asked to spend time in a group context, complete time-limited written projects or visit the client group they will be working with. This is particularly important because, too often in the past, team leaders have been appointed on the basis of what they have done in a non-managerial post, whereas the position of team leader requires a different set of skills.

2.3 SECOND STAGE: BIRTH

2.3 (i) Team tasks

During the first two weeks of the team, at its birth or induction, a number of things have to happen. New team members have to be introduced to the culture of the organisation, the bureaucratic procedures, the geography, the communication and decision-making systems, and then develop a plan of action. Equally importantly, the team members have to let go of their previous jobs, learn something about each other, begin to explore their strengths and weaknesses, and look at how issues of power and leadership will work out.

If this is a new team, all of this will ideally take place during an induction period, which could last from two days to two weeks.

2.3 (ii) Senior management responsibilities

These include:

o planning, monitoring and supervising the birth

o establishing the type of relationship that they plan to have initially with the team

o helping the team locate itself within the wider structure

o identifying the training needs of the team leader.

This is particularly important if this is a first-tier management post.

2.3 (iii) Role of the team doctor

Outside consultants have a number of different functions. The first is to help the team to jell. Among the exercises/activities that consultants can introduce are:

o games and exercises which involve people sharing things about themselves. An example would be a version of musical chairs called 'fruit salad' where there is one less chair than the number of participants who are sitting in a circle. This means that there is one person left in the middle. S/he will call out something that two or more people in the group might have in common, for example 'been to university'. Those who fall in this category have to swap seats and someone else is left chairless and in the middle. They then have to think of, and call out, another category.

o tasks which involve everyone in the group working with everyone else. This has a number of purposes:
  • it helps create group safety
  • it provides the basis for exploring strengths and weaknesses
  • it enables differences to come to the fore which might need to be resolved

o participants being given the opportunity to share negative and positive aspects of their previous posts – what were they sorry to leave and what are they looking forward to in their new jobs? Leaving a job is akin to a small bereavement. Unless the grieving process is finished, feelings from the old job will interfere with the performance of the next one.

o exercises which enable different styles of leadership to be explored. This might involve giving the whole team a task such as 'come up with three main priorities' and then give feedback to the group on how they managed the task. It is always important that the consultant sees his/her role here to help the team leader develop a style of management which will help him/her to get the best out of the team and achieve the task.

o members being given the space to talk about any fears or doubts and how they might be resolved.

Second, consultants can devise exercises which enable group members to identify the different team roles which they are likely to fill and the implications of these choices.

These might range from outdoor activities, such as building a raft to cross a stream, to indoor exercises such as named squares. Here, each person writes their first name on an A4 sheet of paper. These are then placed in a square or rectangle on the floor with one blank sheet in the middle row. Participants then have to stand on someone else's name. The task is to get everyone back onto their own name. The rules are that you cannot move diagonally and you cannot have two people on the same square at once.

In all these cases, the consultant is helping the teams to develop patterns of working and relating and problem solving in ways which they can carry back with them when they start in post.

2.4 THIRD STAGE: INFANCY

2.4 (i) *Team tasks*

These are:

1. To develop the structures which will enable the team to grow. In particular, this involves setting up a series of team meetings with different purposes. These include:

   - **Decision making and communication meetings.** All teams need to have a forum for making decisions and exchanging information about external and internal factors which affect team functioning.
   - **Team learning.** All teams engage daily, via individual members completing tasks or interacting with clients, in a number of pieces of work. Some of these will be done well, some adequately and some, with hindsight, could have been done better. It is possible to learn from both ends of the spectrum by analysing what worked and what didn't.

     Unfortunately, most teams are unable to provide a safe enough environment for members to share their learning. Performance-related pay and performance targets often work against this, setting individuals up in a competitive relationship with each other.

     A good test of whether teams can do team learning is to ask three questions. First, 'Can you talk about something you have done well?' A supplementary question is: 'When did your team last meet to talk about all the things you are doing well?' Second, 'Is it safe enough to admit mistakes?' Third, 'Can the group openly discuss and creatively explore an individual's situation?' Too often, the answer to all three is 'no'. For there to be a 'yes' answer, teams have to have developed a safe space, time and trust and a non-competitive way of working with each other. This requires recognising the need for people to spend time with each other, working arrangements between team members and an appropriate leadership style. These are all discussed in more detail below. The failure to create a learning environment limits not only the possibilities of making the team more effective by utilising all teaching opportunities but also limits what can be done about quality, monitoring stress and increasing productivity.

- **Support.** 'The best figures available indicate that 37 million working days each year are lost because of stress-related illnesses' (Cabinet Office OCMS 1987, p.54). Among the caring professions, doctors, nurses, social workers and teachers all suffered from more than average stress.

  In order to cope with stress all teams need to find a way of giving support to each other. Such support may be informal (morning cup of tea get-together or end of day or shift winding-down sessions) or more formal in terms of time set aside at meetings. Such meetings may also include staff dinners and fun away-days such as a team hike and picnic.

  Often people in teams, when they are asked where they get their main support from, answer that it is from people they share their lives with outside work. This makes these people into unpaid workers of the authority or organisation for whom their partners work. The risk is that this becomes circular because pressures taken home create stress at home which then gets fed back into work.

- **Sensitivity meetings.** These are when the staff meet to sort out communication and emotional blocks which are getting in the way of team functioning. These factors are often referred to as 'hidden agendas' or those things which can't be talked about in the staff meetings but are whispered about in pairs in the toilets afterwards. A good staff team is one where all issues can be resolved openly.

2. To establish a performance review and supervision system. This consists of three parts:

   - a formal supervision structure, which means a meeting every two or three weeks when a staff member and a supervisor look at the member's work in terms of targets met, procedures followed, learning and training needs, difficult areas and emotional support

- a biannual performance appraisal which takes a longer term look at the individual and the wider organisation, what each wants to achieve and what needs to happen for this to occur

- a system to review the team's progress towards meeting its quarterly (or whatever appropriate period) plan. This clearly requires the plans to be formulated in a way that their progress can be measured and monitored – the role of targets and performance indicators.

3. To set up a system which encourages joint working. Teams within which people work on their own or in regular pairs or sub-groups are rarely safe enough for experiences to be shared. Often such teams develop 'in' and 'out' groups where, for example, one shift will blame the other for everything that goes wrong.

One way of getting round this is to set up as many opportunities for shared work as possible so that team members get to work with each other. Not only will this help to share skills but it will make the team feel safer as people come to know and trust each other.

4. Establishing boundary controls. These consist of two parts. The first is clarifying who belongs to which team. Often people are members of a number of work teams. This is particularly true where there are multi-disciplinary work groups. A person might belong to a ward team, a professional team and also be part of a multi-disciplinary work group. It is important to identify core members, that is those whose prime allegiances are to that team or whose membership is essential to its functioning. From this it follows that the team needs to be clear as to who needs to be involved in which part of the team structure.

The same questions apply to volunteers, part-time staff, manual and temporary workers. There needs to be a balance between the need to be involved and the fact that too many people at, for example, team meetings, can make them less productive and safe. Particularly in the case of multi-disciplinary work groups, it is important to disentangle different aspects of each person's work (e.g. their professional input) from how cases are allocated and where their personal support comes from, and to work out appropriate systems so that both these and the team's collective needs are met.

The second aspect of boundary control is that all teams need some way of controlling the through-put of work in terms of what they can manage. Sometimes they will be expected to work to department-wide guidelines, for example staff/patient ratios, but there still needs to be some sort of team control to take account of issues such as staff shortages.

There are a number of schemes which attempt to set up these controls, such as workload management, but these all have to function within a power framework. Teams which can't say 'no' to external demands are teams which often find it difficult to control stress and to develop high-quality work.

There is a balance between resources and output, which means that there is a limit to increased effectiveness unless resources are improved. This will involve teams in being clear as to what work they should be doing, setting priorities, monitoring through-put and negotiating frameworks with senior management and the agencies that supply them with their work.

2.4 (ii) Senior management responsibilities

- o to ensure that the systems are set in place
- o to give support and supervision to the team leader where appropriate.

In practice, few managers get adequate supervision. There is a 'macho' cult which says that if you're good enough to be a manager, then you shouldn't need support. Even where there is supervision it is often very task-orientated – 'Have the performance targets been met?' – rather than enabling the manager to talk through all aspects of his or her work.

2.4 (iii) Role of the team doctor

There are a number of different ways that a consultant can help:

o to set up and run appropriate training courses in areas such as supervisory skills

o to sit in on occasional team meetings as a means of reflecting back to teams how they are handling the task (i.e. to do with work) and maintenance (i.e. to do with team relations) functions of their work.

o as a facilitator of sensitivity meetings or away days where an outsider can usefully provide:

  • a safe space
  • a key to help a team look at how it is working and where it is blocked.

This is often essential in teams which carry a high therapeutic workload, where there is a risk that tension in clients and their families will become reflected in the way the team works.

2.5 FOURTH STAGE: ADOLESCENCE

2.5 (i) Team tasks

At this stage in a group there are often conflicts as team members begin fighting for the space or freedom to develop the work in their own way. Whereas before we looked at the task roles that teams need, the emphasis here is on the maintenance roles, such as those to do with encouragement, gatekeeping or enabling members to have their say, summarising, harmonising, expressing group feeling and tension releasing such as by joking. These positive roles need to be there to cope with dysfunctional roles such as aggression, blocking, competitiveness and withdrawing.

At the start of a team, most people, unless they have been appointed against their will, want to make a good job of it. Over time, though, differences both in ways of doing the work and in personality emerge. Teams need skills to deal with these. Just as in parenthood, when dealing with teenagers, team leaders have choices as to how they tackle these differences. They can decide to be authoritarian ('This is what we will do because I say so'), bureaucratic ('This is the way the department says such problems should be resolved'), laissez-faire ('Sort it yourselves'), democratic centralist ('Let's discuss this and then I will make a decision') or democratic ('This needs to be resolved, what's the best way of organising ourselves to reach a decision?').

Most team leaders recognise the need to be flexible in choice of style, as what the team will need will vary over time. In general, a style which encourages participation from team members will work best as this will enable a team to use its strengths, make members feel involved and thus ensure a greater commitment to work. However, there might well be times when one team member starts underachieving, when a more direct leadership style is called for if the whole team's performance isn't going to suffer. It could be argued that it is still up to the team, collectively, to resolve the issue, but this argument usually fails to take into account the fact that the team has a number of tasks to meet and that overindulgence in its own workings means that the clients or output will suffer.

One function of the team leader is to ensure an appropriate balance between task and maintenance functions. This might mean that s/he takes on specific roles such as compromiser or enables others in the group to do this.

One problem that sometimes arises is where a staff team wishes to work democratically but operates within an authority which has a formal, authoritarian structure where the leader is expected to fill many of the tasks and maintenance roles and is given sole responsible for the team's performance. A solution here is for the team to operate dual structures – a more formal one when facing outward and dealing with the wider agency and a more democratic one when facing inwards and going about their daily work.

At the adolescent stage, then, the team needs to recognise that this is a stage when members are re-negotiating what they are expected to do and how they work with each other. It is a time for re-assessing strengths in the knowledge that has now been gained about the work the team has to do. It is obviously also a time when some team members decide that the work no longer appeals to them or that it has lost its challenge.

The team leader has to find a way, by individual supervision and different team meetings, to enable these re-assessments of the work to take place.

2.5 (ii) Senior management responsibilities

These are to:

o support the team leader

o be aware of the conflicts that might be brewing. A senior manager who only talks to the team manager and uses no other feedback as to how the team is functioning is likely to be given only a partial picture of the team dynamics.

2.5 (iii) Role of the team doctor

The consultant's function is to help the team move forward through this stage. Sometimes difficult feelings will make the team feel unsafe. A number of things might then happen. These include situations where:

o team members seek individual solutions

- members only talk about issues which they feel are safe

- the difficult feelings get projected onto some trivial event which suddenly takes on an undue significance

- people use each other, the organisation and its customers as scapegoats

- cliques exist

- informal power structures develop.

In all these cases the consultant needs to find a way to let the real agendas/issues emerge and be sorted out.

Often because the team leader has become part of the problem, the doctor has to take over this role temporarily. This, if done well, provides a safe space for the team to begin moving through the issues.

2.6 FIFTH STAGE: MATURITY

2.6 (i) Team tasks

The tasks are to have achieved the characteristics of a well-functioning team. These include:

- clear objectives which are accepted by all team members

- boundaries as to who is and who is not a team member. This is important in terms of part-time staff, people who work in more than one team, and support staff such as office workers, cleaners and domestics

- skills of members acknowledged and a way of working which utilises their strengths

- structure for making decisions and resolving differences

- systems to ensure effective communication and to effectively review, monitor and evaluate the team's work

- an underlying system of beliefs or values, including anti-discriminatory practices, which guide the team members in the way they approach their work

- an appropriate mix of individuals so as to fill the internal team roles and to have the necessary skills to meet the work demands

- an effective gatekeeper with the wider organisation and with other agencies. This is necessary to prevent overload, ensure adequate resources from competition with other teams, clarify the team's role within the wider department and guarantee external recognition of the team's work. This is important both to ensure the team's future and to give feedback to the team on its efforts

o being action focused. It is little use having a superbly democratic team which devotes its major efforts to resolving internal differences if the work for which the team was set up doesn't get done

o good and appropriate leadership which enables the team to meet both its task and maintenance needs

o an acknowledgement of individuals and what they can contribute

o ways of letting go of departing members and welcoming new members.

Departing members need a process which adequately reflects their contribution to the team and which helps them move on to their next situation. New people need to be welcomed and introduced to how the team works formally and informally. Also, the team has to look at itself to make sure that it is creating a space for the entrant to fill.

Particular teams will also have more precise needs if they are to work well. Multi-disciplinary teams, for example, will need a complex system of organisation which enables the work, professional and personal needs of the team members to be met.

Therapeutic teams are more likely to require forms of group supervision of individual members and of the team as a whole if they are to be able to work with the different levels of feelings which are at the core of their work.

Task-orientated teams brought together for a set number of meetings to complete a project will have to have a much tighter structure around issues such as time management, if their work is to be effective.

One other thing that all teams need is an understanding of power. If they are to be effective, they will need to be aware of their power to effect change, to gather resources and implement action, and also to recognise who wields what kind of power within the team. One way teams become ineffective is when the official and unofficial power systems are at variance. This might be because of an inappropriate selection of a team manager. Problems can then arise where the rest of the team might recognise one of their own members as having greater knowledge or job skill. Problems also exist where a team member has negative power to sabotage unless his or her wishes are taken into account. This negative power might come from a personality base or from a power position centred on race, gender, politics, trade unionism or alliance to a particular departmental action.

It is important to recognise that this negative power might be a positive response to sexist, racist or ageist policies within a team.

2.6 (ii) Senior management responsibilities

These are simply to help by giving the necessary support and supervision. The risk is that a well-functioning team is left well alone. However, unless it continues to be stretched and to set itself new goals, then it will descend into middle and old age.

2.6 (iii) Role of the team doctor

One of the signs of a mature team is that they welcome the opportunity to review their performance, similar to an annual medical check-up.

The role of the consultant is to help the team review their progress, look at their internal functioning and establish new goals and targets for the next period of work. The function is one of fine tuning, particularly of looking for ways of releasing energies that might have got blocked because of team routines. This might well involve the team having fun through games or by producing plays, for example.

2.7 SIXTH STAGE: MIDDLE AGE

2.7 (i) Team tasks

This stage is reached when a team has been working for a while. People have come and gone, team members have developed their own ways of working, leadership styles might have failed to adapt to changing circumstances and systems for maintaining a group focus have fallen into disuse.

An example would be where a team is still continuing to tackle its work in the same way, even though the nature of the work or the priorities as seen by others have changed. There might well be pressures on the team to increase its workload and the gatekeeper function might have failed to keep a check on these.

Under the pressure of the extra work, team meetings will be poorly attended, supervision sessions will be skipped and the team leader will get drawn into helping out with the work rather than ensuring that the necessary managerial functions of planning, resource allocation, reviewing and monitoring work are carried out.

Under these pressures individuals will develop their own survival mechanisms, which might be at the expense of other team members.

Alternatively, the team might have started drifting. If there has been little change in either the team membership or the work that the team does, everything might have slowed down and become routine. Team meetings will become primarily a gossip session, quality standards without external monitoring will have fallen, and the team members will have lost their enthusiasm and have come to see their work as just another job.

A different scenario would be where a team leader started with a style of leadership which has outlived its usefulness. In one case a new team leader who took over a drifting team put herself in a very central position and held nearly all the reins of power. While this, at the beginning, gave the team a much needed sense of structure, after five years it had sapped the team's initiative and the team was looking to an external saviour to help create new space. This need for emotional and decision-making space had become expressed in the desire for a new building, that is more physical space, which was safer to talk about.

Also what often happens is that, with staff turnover, key team roles are lost. People tend to appoint people like themselves, so that if people have reached a stage of working comfortably together they are unlikely to appoint anyone who is an innovator or a radical. Without someone filling that role, however, teams tend to drift into compromised complacency.

On other occasions, it might well be the nurturing roles that are lost so that no one in the team arranges the informal support systems such as morning or afternoon tea breaks, necessary for the maintenance part of team functioning. In some teams the leader will originally have taken the lion's share of the team roles but, over time, will have allowed some to lapse or will have delegated them unclearly.

As regards the team leader, s/he will, without supervision, support and training, find it difficult over a period of years to keep up the same level of motivation.

2.7 (ii) Senior management responsibilities

Regrettably, teams which have begun to stagnate often score highly in bureaucratic organisations because they make no demands on the rest of the structure. High-performing teams or teams which perform so poorly that they endanger the organisations' welfare are bureaucratic anathema because they disturb its equilibrium. In both cases, part of the responsibility of the falling off in performance rests with the management in the wider structure. This is because the situation should have been picked up earlier via supervision or the monitoring of management information returns. This, in turn, implies that the team has agreed measurable performance objectives.

What senior management needs to do, therefore, is first, to recognise that something is wrong, second, to analyse its cause and, third, to initiate corrective action.

This is often easier said than done if the problem rests with the team manager. Well-established leaders accrue a lot of legitimate and interpersonal power, and many senior managers shy away from tackling them. This is one of the times when team doctors are called in (see 'The killing fields' in Section II, p.92).

2.7 (iii) Role of the team doctor

The first role of the consultant at this stage is to help the team to stand back and look at how it is working. A second task is to help the team redefine its aims and objectives. A third function is to help rebuild team structures. These will include gatekeeping functions, such as helping to set up a work load management system, re-establishing the pattern of team meetings and what needs to happen to make them effective and feeding in new ideas about ways of working. The advantage of an outside consultant is that s/he can be a carrier of good practice from one workplace to another. Often the team will have lost the perspective of what the work looks like from the viewpoint of the client, patient or customer. The consultant can enable the leader to look at her/his job and the roles s/he should fill and enable the team to see how it goes about its work, helping both develop more effective and efficient ways of doing so.

A useful exercise is a SWOT analysis, where the team looks at its strengths, weaknesses, opportunities and threats. The first two categories relate primarily to the team's internal functioning, the last two to its external environment.

Overall, the job is to give the team feedback, either to help it to take back control of itself and re-establish safe boundaries and operating systems, or to get people to realise that their standards have slipped and to acknowledge the need to improve them.

What often makes this difficult is that, as team meetings have fallen off, the team as a whole becomes a less safe space. Team members begin to operate in sub-groups, to carve out space for themselves in the office or staff room, right down to ownership of the tea mugs. The less safe the team is, the more difficult it is to review practice or to learn from mistakes. This is particularly true where individuals are encouraged to compete with each other. It might well separate the sheep from the goats but the sheep keep their skills to themselves and everyone fails to learn from the skills of the goats. So an additional function of the consultant is to help make the team a safe place again.

In the case of the team leader who was being too dogmatic it was necessary to find a way of releasing space for the rest of the team while not destroying her strengths.

2.8 SEVENTH STAGE: OLD AGE

2.8 (i) Team tasks

As in the case of middle age, we are dealing here with a team that has lost its way and is no longer coping with its tasks.

At this age illnesses tend to be serious for a team. The effect is that some part of the team stops functioning or works in such a maladaptive way that the future of the whole team is threatened.

Examples of this may be a team leader who, because of some personal crisis, no longer behaves appropriately; an individual team member attacking other team members in a way that sours all the working relationships; or a team whose structures are paralysed by a very frightening patient.

A different form of serious illness occurs when excessive team pressures overwhelm the team's defences and people feel that there is no alternative but to bail out and seek alternative jobs.

Alternatively, senility can creep up on a team. This can take a number of different forms:

o The team may have lost its purpose entirely. Often the task it has been set up to do has fundamentally changed and the team has not altered to cope with the new conditions.

o The team leaders may have been there for too long a time. They might have grown old in the job and are simply time serving while they wait for retirement. Or because of the structure in which they work, there is no room to move on and so they are forced to stay on against their will. Similarly, some team leaders realise they should move on but personal circumstances militate against it. In all of these cases team leaders are likely to become embittered and to sour team relationships.

2.8 (ii) Senior management responsibilities

In the case of the team having lost its way, the line manager should have been aware of what was going wrong through his/her monitoring of the situation. Then s/he needed to have stepped in and set up the team meetings or individual supervision sessions with the team manager to put the team back on the tracks.

Where team functions are changing, the role of the line manager is to plan the management of change together with the team to set and get agreement to targets, check resources and then monitor what happens.

With ageing team leaders or with those who have become the team dinosaurs, the line manager should have addressed the problem at an earlier stage. One way of doing this is through some form of annual performance appraisal where people have an opportunity to review their work within the team and the organisation and to set themselves targets for the coming year.

If someone is stuck they could be offered inducements to take early retirement, move sideways or even, on occasions, downwards on a protected salary. Alternatively, they could be promoted up-wards to a non-essential job (the role, sometimes, of a vice-presi-dency or of a vague research and development brief) or have it made clear that there is little future for them in the organisation and to offer 'out-placement planning'.

Unfortunately, not all line managers do what is expected of them and sometimes, either through lack of experience or because they don't want to confront the issue, they delegate the task to the team doctor.

2.8 (iii) Role of the team doctor

Where the problem is the team leader (the dead weight of a charis-matic leader can stifle the rest of the team), one role for the doctor is to enable the leader to see that it is time to move on or to radically alter their style and/or attitude.

Where the team has lost its purpose, the doctor needs to help it see where it has gone and, from this basis, help it plot a way to where it needs to go if it is going to survive. This is often a fairly painful process, as one of the reasons why teams stay stuck is that they perceive the changes as something that will threaten their working ethos, their individual work practices or their working conditions. There are times when all of these are true perceptions and people need either to look at how they can minimise the cost or to make the painful decision that they no longer want to work in that organisa-tion. Sometimes, there is a third path, where the team members decide that what they are working for is worth fighting to keep, and what they want the team doctor to do is to help them analyse and utilise their resources to best re-motivate themselves.

3. SECTION II
Team Doctoring

3.1 OUTLINE OF SECTION II

Section II looks at key issues around the role of a team doctor and at the knowledge, practical skills and techniques which are useful to have when working with teams. It is divided into three sections:

3.2 WHO CAN DOCTOR?

(i) The team leader

(ii) Someone else in the organisation

(iii) An outside consultant

(iv) The power of the doctor

(v) Looking after the doctor

(vi) When not to team build

3.3 TEAM PROCESSES AND GAMES

(i) Team processes

(ii) Team games

3.4 TECHNIQUES

(i) Diagnosis

(ii) The present problems

(iii) Moving the team on

3.2 WHO CAN DOCTOR?

3.2 (i) The team leader

The advantage of the team leader taking responsibility for reviewing a team's performances are, first, that s/he knows the team members and, ideally, through supervision will have some idea of their strengths and weaknesses. The second reason is that the team leader is responsible for the team and is exercising a clear management function. The third advantage is that the team leader should be in the position of being able to assess the team's level of functioning in relation to the wider organisation's standards and objectives.

There are, however, disadvantages. The first of these is that the team leader can be part of the team's problem – there may be disharmony, for example, because the team leader has his or her favourites among team members. The second reason is that teams need meetings with structures and rules different from those to do with business matters, if they are going to be safe venues to resolve team difficulties. A team leader might not have the skills or personality to create the atmosphere where staff feel able to be honest with each other. Finally, the team leader might have got so embedded in his or her formal role that s/he doesn't find it possible to stand aside and let a different structure emerge.

For all of these reasons, a team leader is most appropriate when the team is reviewing their work and planning new objectives. It is least appropriate when the team has problems to do with interpersonal relationships.

3.2 (ii) Someone else in the organisation

This might be someone from the personnel, training or staff development sections, a senior manager, a fellow team leader or someone employed in an advisory capacity.

The advantages of using a person in this position are, first, that they are independent of the team, second, that they will have knowledge about the wider organisation and, third, that they might well have group work skills.

Against this there would be the fact that the team might feel that what it discloses may be fed back to senior management and that this might affect the level of trust. There is no guarantee that people will have the necessary skills. There is the fear that, if a team calls in someone from within the organisation, it may be taken as a sign of incompetency. Finally, if someone from higher up comes in, this is likely to undermine the authority of the team leader.

Therefore someone else in the organisation is likely to work best when the issues are to do with the team's relation to the wider structure, or where there is a pre-negotiation and contracting stage to establish rules about confidentiality and when the person's power base in relation to the team is clarified.

3.2 (iii) An outside consultant

The advantages of outside consultants are their independence and their skills. These should make the team sessions safer provided that there is a clear contract between the consultant and the team. This is particularly important when the person who employs the consultant is not a team member. The disadvantage is that the consultant will be less clued into the background against which the team works. Also, if, as a result of the team building sessions, it become necessary to represent the team's needs to higher interests, the consultant might not have the same access that someone from within the authority would have.

An outside consultant is likely to be necessary when the team is confronting 'maintenance' problems which include the team leader and where safety is a crucial issue.

3.2 (iv) The power of the doctor

The doctor needs to be aware of his/her bases of power and how they relate to the team and its power bases.

The doctor's power might come from a combination of his/her professionalism, inter-personal skills, charisma, energy, role as a doctor, reputation and how well s/he conforms to existing perceptions of who is powerful within the culture/sub-cultures that the group members belong to.

Therefore, in a stereotypical sense, being white, male, middle-class, young, heterosexual and able-bodied will conform to what many people see as being the characteristics of powerful people in society at large. In some sub-cultures, however, these would be seen as negative attributes either because of the experience of oppression or because other attributes were more highly prized. A trainer's power, therefore, will depend, to some extent, on how his/her attributes are valued within the group.

This is also dependent on how trainers themselves understand and deal with these perceptions. It has often been noted, for example, that men and women have very different managerial styles. Men are said to prefer a transactional leadership style which is 'more formal, status-conscious, directive and controlling', while women prefer a more transformational style which is 'empowering, sharing, consultative and collaborative' (Alims-Metcalfe 1993, p.26). If these gender differences were also true of facilitators, then it can be seen that a male facilitator who responded to perceptions of his male role in a transactional style might well end up emphasising the more negative aspects of the role.

What is important for the facilitator is to be aware of his/her effect on the group, both in terms of perceptions and interventions. This is especially important, for example, if a white male trainer is working with a predominantly female group in which there are a couple of black workers. In cases like this, it might be particularly important for the trainer to co-lead the day with a female black colleague, or at the very least that the whole team is given a say in the selection of the facilitator.

3.2 (v) Looking after the doctor

Whoever takes on the role needs to be aware that the rule 'physician heal thyself' is particularly true in the case of team doctoring. Team doctoring is an immensely tiring activity. It is, in fact, like doing a non-stop six to eight hour family session. This is why it often makes sense for team doctors to work in pairs, to have somebody not only to give support, but also with whom to check out what is going on in the room. The team doctor has to listen not only to the surface agendas, but also to the group dynamics and what might be going on for each of the different individuals in the group at any one time.

The most important preparation that a team doctor needs is to give him- or herself the space to listen and to work with what the group brings up. Agendas and issues often emerge during the course of a session, and it is important to pay attention to the issues that the team indicates that it needs to work on. Therefore it becomes important for the team doctor to be someone who can work flexibly and adapt the agenda for the day as needs arise.

3.2 (vi) When not to team build

If the team or members in it are involved in a grievance procedure, keep clear. The power to resolve things in the team has been transferred elsewhere in the organisation. Thus it is only possible to air some of the grievances because others are subjudice – the day is full of hidden agendas, with few opportunities for constructive action.

3.3 TEAM PROCESSES

3.3 (i) Team processes

The team doctor has to make the day safe to start with. Unless the team feels that the overall climate is one in which risks can be taken, then people will disappear into their defensive stances.

The setting for the day, therefore, is very important. It needs to be a place which demonstrates to the team that they are cared for – for example, a nice room, or a day out somewhere. Arrangements have to be made to avoid interruption.

The first stage needs to be a *warm-up*. One way of starting this is to get everyone at the beginning of the session to introduce themselves, say who they are (for the doctor's benefit), why they think the day has been called and what they want out of it.

This has a number of purposes:

o to get everyone to enter into the day and begin to leave behind things or worries not directly pertinent to the session

o to establish an informal rule that everyone speaks

o to enable the director to hear how much discussion there has been about the workshop, what sources of tension exist within and between individuals and what degree of commitment the team members are bringing to the session. All of these will help the director decide at what pace to work with the group.

Part of creating the safe structure is to set up a number of rules for the day, which could be seen as a contract. These might include rules about confidentiality (both in terms of what team members say but also in terms of with whom the doctor can share her/his notes from the day), agreement as to break and finish times, paying attention to anti-discriminatory issues, and consensus about a draft agenda for the day. The agenda might have been provisionally agreed beforehand but it still needs to be checked out at the beginning, and again at different parts of the day as the action unfolds.

The next part of the day will be the *diagnostic* stage, finding some agreement about what is happening in the team. This might involve, for example, taking a team history.

Following on from this would be the *action*, looking at what needs to be changed and finding a way of doing this. Part of the action and/or diagnostic stages needs to be done in small groups. Part of team building is developing trust, and one way of doing this is by working with everyone else in the team. Working in continually changing small groups is a way of achieving this.

The next stage will be the *learning*, where the team takes on board what new knowledge they have gained and considers how this will be maintained back in the workplace. This stage often needs to be handed back to the team leader to run, because s/he is the person who will have responsibility for ensuring that it happens back in the workplace. Doing this provides an opportunity for the team and its leaders:

o to own the solution

o to practise the new roles learnt from the day, and to help ensure that they will be used when the team returns to work.

The final stage is the *ending*, the sharing between people of what they have got from the day. This might entail, for example, space for everyone to spend time with every other person in the team, telling them what they have learnt about them from the day. This could be followed by people in a circle sharing a final thought.

Breaks during the day have an important symbolic function. It is time when the team can literally, as well as symbolically, feed itself. The need for team doctoring is often a sign that the team has stopped looking after itself. Food is a way of feeding, sharing and caring. Therefore team meals, ideally where everyone brings something to share, are a way of expressing this and indicating to the team the importance of the maintenance role.

Equally important is the *bedside manner* of the doctor. The doctor is a role model for the team, the way a leader should function. Therefore the doctor needs to demonstrate listening skills and care for the individual as well as task skills in terms of managing the day and helping the team achieve a set of relationships which can move them forward.

3.3 (iii) Games

Games are an important part of team building work. There are a number of books (for example Jennings, 1986) which describe a wide variety of games.

They can be used for different stages of the process. At the beginning they might range from those to do with communalities (i.e. looking for things team members have in common) to 'getting to know you' exercises (e.g. using masks to show the face you don't normally show to people).

During the day, games can be used to:

o create energy after breaks

o help diagnosis (e.g. a trust-holding game, when the team allowed someone to fall, served as a sign of how dangerous the team was)

o build up trust

o explore how teams tackle tasks

o simply have fun. This is often an aspect that teams stuck in middle-age need o add new dimensions, such as touch, to team relationships.

In using games, the doctor needs to be aware of:

o the safety of the team members

o the preparedness of people to be involved, since different games require varying levels of trust and safety

o the purpose of a particular game at any one time

o the cultural backgrounds of different course members.

Some teams will have come with an attitude, such as 'We're not here to play silly buggers', and there is little point in trying to foist a game onto them. It is necessary to start with the culture that the team has and then to find a way to move it on. The doctor has to find a way of using the team's strength, even if it is initially expressed negatively. In the end, the team is more powerful than the doctor, and if confronted at the wrong time or in the wrong way it will simply shut up shop.

3.4 TECHNIQUES

3.4 (i) Diagnosis

The first task of the doctor is to establish what the team's problems are. The first attempt to do this is at the initial stage of consultation. The team representative says, 'We would like you to come and spend time with the team because we have a problem with x.'

However, is 'x' the real problem? We all know that in medical consultations with GPs, psychological difficulties are dressed up in physical symptoms, because that is the acceptable language for both patient and doctor.

Similarly with teams, it is easier and more acceptable to say, 'We have extremely difficult children we are finding hard to control' rather than 'Our staff team is all over the place, the children sense that and they are creating problems we aren't cohesive enough to deal with.'

So the initial task is to check whether the presenting symptoms are masking underlying difficulties.

(A) INITIAL IMPRESSIONS

Just as a patient in a surgery will convey information by the way s/he presents him/herself, so will staff teams.

As they come into a room the team doctor might look out for:

o how easy people are with each other; how warm the greetings are

- whether people remain in small sub-groups or whether there is a lot of intermingling

- the degree of rigidity, such as people having their own seats or seating order

- the effect that the team leader has on the group as a whole, or parts of it, by his or her presence

- how punctual people are.

This information will help the consultant pick up an atmosphere and gain some idea of how the team organises itself.

(B) THE FIRST QUESTION

A good way to start a team building day is to get everyone to introduce themselves and say what they want from the day and how they come to be there.

The answers will help the consultant find out how many people want to be there, the different expectations that team members have, how easy people feel in speaking out in the group and whose voice carries most weight.

(C) TAKING A HISTORY

In a conventional medical examination, one of the first tasks for the doctor is to carry out a detailed history of the patient. In this case, the same can be done for a team.

There are a number of different ways of doing this. One way is to get people in the group to describe what it was like when they joined. This exercise starts with the oldest member (i.e. the one longest in the team), who describes the team members in the group when s/he began, where the team was based, what its aims were, how the team organised the work and the way the team members worked with one another.

The next oldest team member then comes forward and describes how the team appeared when s/he first joined it and how it has changed. Other people in the team have an opportunity to ask questions whenever they want.

An alternative way of doing this is for the facilitator to take the team back to the time when the problems began, and then ask the team members to describe what has happened since then. The facilitator records key points on large sheets of paper.

This process enables the team to put together a common history; people often find for the first time how and why different events have the importance they have. One of the main advantages that the team doctor has is that s/he can always play the role of the outsider and ask naive questions, such as 'How does this work in your team?' or 'Why did that happen?'

This is often a therapeutic exercise, especially if people feel that their distress is being listened to. It also allows the consultant to put together a picture of the way the team was built, to consider the role of outside factors such as senior management decisions, the importance and style of different leaders, the development of informal rules and to see how staff team practices have emerged.

(D) ROAD MAPS

When using road maps with individual clients, counsellors ask the person to show their life as a road with roundabouts, crossroads, detours and the like. It is a way of getting people to look back on their life to see where they got stuck, where they made crucial decisions and the effect of the choices arrived at.

For the staff team, the task is similar. Either people may be asked to draw their own road maps of how they came to join the team and share these with other participants, or people may be divided into sub-groups of three to five people, and asked to use the idea of a road map to agree on their view of the team's history. The maps can then be passed around until a common history is agreed on.

(E) DRAWING THE TEAM HISTORY

Similar to the above process, the team can be asked to draw a collective picture of their team's history. This often works best if people are asked to depict key incidents symbolically.

One advantage of this method is that the history can be pinned up on the wall as a reminder. The exercise can be repeated at the end of the team building period, with people either being asked to draw the team as it is now or how it will be in the future. This can then be put on a different wall and contrasted with the first attempt.

Again, the process of how the team completes the task will give the consultant insight into how the team members work in the roles they adopt.

(F) DRAMA

The team can be asked to devise a short play showing key scenes from its history. One way of doing this is to open with a discussion to agree on the main points. The group is sub-divided, with each smaller group taking responsibility for presenting a scene. This will only work as a warm up if the team comes to the session energised and fairly cohesive.

(G) SETTING THE TEAM TO 'DOCTOR' ITSELF

The team can be divided into sub-groups and asked to come up with the list of symptoms they see in the team which they would want to discuss with a team doctor. These are recorded on flip charts. The actual doctor or consultant can then ask questions such as, 'How long have these problems existed? How severe are they? Which part of the team feels them most?' The team can then be asked to suggest solutions. One team came up with euthanasia, long term sick leave, retirement and a long holiday, which gave a very clear message as to that team's state of health.

(H) STORY TELLING

The team can be asked to tell their history in the form of a story, such as a fairy tale. One person starts off, then different people pick up the story and continue it.

3.4 (ii) Present problems

Once there has been an initial diagnosis, some history taken, a contract agreed, and perhaps some introductory warm-up exercise, it becomes important to establish what is happening in the team at the moment. Where is it going? What are its dynamics? Where has it got stuck? Where are the power issues? It is possible to get to this by discussion in a whole team or sub-team grouping. Discussion is, however, a limited diagnostic tool in comparison with:

(A) SCULPTING

In sculpting, the group is asked to form itself physically around a concept or issue of the doctor's choice. This decision will be based on what appears most relevant to look at. Therefore, if it appears important to explore the relationship between the team and the outside world, team members might be asked to show this.

If the internal dynamics of the team were important to explore, then the team might be asked to depict itself as a family.

In one case, looking at the relationship between a probation team and its wider structure, people were chosen to represent key group-ings within the team, such as secretarial, reception, workers and management. The other people then became the different agencies, such as the courts, clients, other staff in other teams, senior manage-ment etc. If, for example, the clients were seen to be exerting a lot of pressure on the workers, this was shown in the sculpt by the person representing the client leaning against the person representing the worker.

By doing this, the team could see and agree as to where the pressures were coming from and how this was beginning to affect relationships between people within the team.

Basing a sculpt around a family is a particularly useful method for exploring team relationships. One way of sculpting this is for the consultant to ask one of the team members to choose a role for the others and then place them so that how and where they are put indicates the relationships that exist between them. Thus, in a sculpt around the idea of a family, if two people were seen to be like mother and daughter, the daughter might be asked to kneel beside the mother. If the relationship was seen as a protective one, then the mother might have her arm round the daughter to indicate this.

Once everyone is in position – and a space needs to be left for the sculptor – the sculptor is asked to double for each of the team members. This means that s/he puts her hand on each person's shoulder and speaks as if she is that person, e.g. 'In this family I am the daughter. I don't always like this role as my brothers seem to expect me to tidy up after them.'

Once the doubling has finished, everyone in the group is given the opportunity to say how they feel about the role they have been given and the words attributed to them.

Once the first sculpt has been done, the facilitator should check whether anyone else has a very different perception of team relationships and, if the answer is yes, then this person should be given the opportunity to resculpt the team.

As will no doubt be clear, the doctor has to give some thought as to whom to choose as the sculptor. Ideally the person should be intuitive, have sufficient group respect that they will be listened to, be prepared to take risks and be able to cope with possible criticisms of his/her decisions. The process of sculpting helps the staff team to explore the issues which are confronting it. It is a form of x-ray, a way of seeing beneath the surface, which a discussion often fails to achieve. The doubling often helps people to say things that they were finding difficult to say directly.

Another example of sculpting was in a team which was closing down a series of residential homes. At the end of this process the team was left with a lot of grief, which the day had been set up to deal with. The team was asked to use the furniture to sculpt the arrangement for the different homes.

On each home (or chair) the doctor placed a number of smarties. The team went collectively around each chair where each smartie became one of the residents who had lived there and the team shared their memories, good and bad, of him or her.

From the consultant's viewpoint, a sculpt enables her to see how issues are seen by teams and, from the way the team builds the sculpt, it gives a further insight into the team's dynamics.

The sculpt serves as an opening which can then lead on to an action phase. In the case of external pressures, people can begin looking at what might need to happen to help the team deal with the stress. In the case of a family team sculpt, people might begin experimenting with different roles.

(B) SOCIOMETRY

This is a similar tool for helping a consultant to look at a team's innards. Here the consultant asks people to move to indicate the relationships that exist between team members. An example would be, 'Could you please put your hand on the shoulder of the person that you would turn to if you had a work problem in the group?' A series of questions like this will enable the team and the facilitator to see the different roles that people play.

Clearly, in a technique like this it becomes very important for the team doctor to pay attention to the feelings that people have when they are chosen and, even more importantly, the feelings of the people who are not chosen and feel left out.

(C) USING A CASE HISTORY

A different way of working is to ask the team to choose a client or problem that they have at the moment. The consultant can then use this in a variety of different ways:

- **Discussion.** S/he can ask questions such as, 'For whom is this a problem? Why is it a problem? For how long has it been one?', and so on. The answers will give some indication of how the team runs, and why this has become a problem for which people.

- **The empty chair.** It is likely that the 'problem' will not only reflect a real issue but will also be acting as a projection for feelings within the team. One way of getting at this is to put a chair in the centre of the room and to ask people to position themselves so that where they end up reflects how they feel about the problem and whom, in relation to the problem, they want to be close to. This sculpt can then be built on by asking each person to make a statement to the chair (i.e. the problem) as to how they feel about it and what they would like to see happen.

- **Making the problem come alive.** If the problem is a person, the group could role play the history of that person's involvement with the team. This would be done by taking key scenes and re-enacting what happened. By using role reversal and discussion, the doctor can get the team to look at the issues and the feelings that lie behind them.

If the problem is to do with something more bureaucratic, for example a communication breakdown, it again becomes possible to re-create that situation in the room, see how it was tackled and examine alternative ways it could have been dealt with.

o **Creative expression.** Another way of using a case history or problem is to ask the group to find a way of showing or enacting the situation they are having difficulty with. A group of hospital managers, when asked this at the beginning of a workshop, graphically set a waste paper bin on fire and produced a hose beside it; the group was ready to explode and the aim of the day was to find a way of defusing it.

(D) POCKET SCULPTING

As the name implies, this simply involves people using whatever is in their pockets, handbags or in the room to portray a particular situation. The situation could be the team, the support system in the team or the team's relationship with other organisations.

Insights come from the answers to questions that the doctor can ask. Therefore, if s/he were interested in team membership the question might be: 'Who else could have been in the team?' If the issue were team relationships the questions might be: 'Why have you chosen these objects to represent particular people?' and 'What does the relationship between the objects indicate?'

It is possible to use pocket sculpting as a tool for a whole team building session. People are asked individually to depict the team, then to pair up with another team member and agree a new sculpt. The pair then have to find another pair, share their sculpts and agree on a new one, until the whole team has reached an agreed consensus on how the team members are seen and what their relationship is with one another.

The team doctor, during this and any of the other exercises, is concerned with the task, but more importantly with the process, the way the team tackles the task. Therefore, the doctor needs to have in mind all the time, a concept of what a healthy team needs (e.g. clear aims and objectives; appropriate leadership; a system of supervising, monitoring and evaluating the team's work; a way of handling team relationships, etc).

3.5 (iii) Moving the team on

(A) INTRODUCTION

Once the doctor and the team have diagnosed the problem, they then need to find a way to help move the team on.

At this stage, there is often a feeling of gloom and doom as team members experience in a heightened form all the problems they are confronted with on a regular basis. If this is a two-day workshop and this stage is reached at the end of the first day, people will often go away feeling very despondent. However, this is a necessary stage because there is little motivation to carry through the change unless the team feels its despair. In the past, the team has known there is something wrong but has preferred to live with it rather than risk change.

If a team isn't working well, it is likely that interpersonal relationships/communications have become unstuck somewhere. However, it is also the case that the team either does not have or has lost the skills/mechanisms to tackle the problems. There is no point in the doctor sorting out the problems without building in the problem-solving machinery. If this doesn't happen then any cure will be short term and the team will become dependent upon the doctor for regular courses of injections.

Listed below are some of the ways that a consultant can tackle this task.

(B) TASK SETTING

One way of helping a team to work is to give them a task to do, to stop it at key stages and to get the group to look at how they are tackling it. The task can be unreal, that is, not work orientated; for example, 'Put yourself into a group so that everyone is touching and being touched by everyone else.' Or it can be real; for example, 'Let us assume this is one of your team meetings – what might we be discussing?'

The main advantages of an unreal task is that by working on something different, it helps the team to see more clearly the processes that they use or don't use in their workplace. The main disadvantage is that this insight has then to be translated into the workplace situation and acted on there. Unreal tasks range from a simple ten minute exercise to week long outward bound courses.

The advantages of real tasks are that they are immediately relevant; the disadvantage is that because this is the terrain in which the problem lies, it is difficult sometimes for the team to stand back and see what is going on.

In both cases, the job of the doctor is to help the group reflect on how they are tackling the issue, to look at the shortcomings that they have and to help them move on to new ways of working.

The particular tasks will vary from team to team. It might be the case, for example, that team roles are the issue; it might be a team in which there are a lot of ideas but no-one takes responsibility for ensuring that they are carried through or is prepared to work on an idea they haven't thought of. In this case, the doctor might ask the team to do a task which requires completion within a short time period. Alternatively, s/he could use one of the different team questionnaires that are available which analyse team roles.

(C) USING THE GROUP SKILLS

The doctor can always let the group help in the diagnosis and solution. This is important if the team is to own the problem. One way of doing this is by using the group's strength. Hence in working with family therapists, it makes sense to see the team as a dysfunctional family; the team can be asked to show this by a sculpt, and then the team members, in pairs, are asked for the advice they would give to this family if they were the therapists. It is possible to take this further by having two of the 'therapists' sit away from the group, as if behind a one-way mirror, and for the rest to tackle the task, which the therapists then comment on. This not only gives insight into the team's functioning through the therapists' eyes, but at a different level through the interaction between the 'therapists' and the 'family members'. These insights are likely to be in terms of power, individual agendas, projections from one team member onto another, problem solving within the team etc.

If the team were a group of computer analysts then a systems approach might be more appropriate.

(D) THE KILLING FIELDS

One particular area where the doctor might need to intervene is where the team leader is the problem; the doctor then has to decide whether they need to be killed off, metaphorically speaking of course.

When building a team the selection of the leader is all important, so when a team malfunctions, one of the likely causes is that something has happened to the leader. In a medical analogy, if the body isn't functioning as it should, then there is always the chance that it's a sign that the mind isn't right; stress can lead to ulcers, and there is little point in healing the ulcer without reducing the stress.

There are a number of reasons why a team leader might not be performing as well as s/he should:

- o a lack of training to do the job

- o a lack of interpersonal skills

- o an inability to delegate

- o burn out

- o waiting for retirement

- o seen it all before

- threatened by change or by new dynamic staff

- lack of external support

- a shortage of resources

- having favourites among the staff.

The first thing a doctor needs to do is to diagnose what the fault is. This might have been suggested by the commissioning person, if a senior manager; for example, 'So and so is having problems with their team – can you sort it out?.' The problem might be, of course, the lack of support and supervision given by the senior manager, who is expecting the consultant to do the job for him/her. If, however, it becomes clear as the day proceeds that the manager is a serious part of the team's problem, what can the consultant do?

There are a number of options:

- It can be tackled within the context of the day. This is by far the best approach as it will be within the boundaries of the day's contract with the team. A day which energises the team, works through blocks and allows new ideas to flow will often recharge the team leader and help him/her recapture their earlier enthusiasm.

- One way the role of the team manager can be explored is to ask the team to carry out a task within which it becomes clear that the team leader isn't using his or her power or position constructively. The doctor can share this observation with the team. This will only work, however, if the manager wants to change and is able to accept criticism in front of his or her team.

- If the leader wants to change but doesn't feel confident about starting this in full view of the team, then the team doctor can use breaks, or set members other tasks, to provide space to counsel the manager. The risks are that if done in view of others, they will quite rightly want to know what was discussed and, if done secretly, then the doctor is having a different arrangement with the team leader than with other members. This is unlikely to have been part of the contract for the day.

- Alternatively, the doctor can consciously take over running part of the day so as to provide a role model for the leader, who then needs to be given time to practise the new skills before the end of the session. This happened, for example, during an Area Child Protection Committee training day where one of the agenda items was the (lack of) chairing skills of the chairperson.

o Finally, the leader could agree the need for further skills training to take place at a later date. Again, if possible, this should be agreed with the team as a whole because otherwise there is a risk of them seeing something happening with the manager which they might not see as being in their interests; this might work against team unity.

Therefore, the consultant has to find a way of helping the team leader assume his or her managerial function within the context of what was contracted with the team. It is no use leaving the team with an ineffective leader or any progress will soon be lost.

Real problems exist when it becomes clear that it is time for the leader to go, or for their role radically to change. It may be that they have been there too long or are just sitting out time. It may be that they have been promoted so far above their ability that no amount of training will make any appreciable difference. This is an example of the Peter principle, where people are promoted to their level of incompetence. The solution is often to promote people further, to the level where they are likely to do least damage to the organisation.

If the doctor is an outside consultant, s/he has only advisory, and not line, power. S/he can't actually fire or promote staff. Therefore s/he has to find an alternative strategy. One way is to let the team tackle a task so that it becomes clear what effect the team leader is having.

This can be shared in a one-to-one situation with the leader so that s/he can see it for themselves. Sometimes it then becomes possible to let the team complete the task with the leader being put in the role of an observer, seeing the benefits that can flow from his/her absence. If the leader can accept that it is time for them to move on or to delegate a lot of their legitimate power down the team, then the task of the facilitator is to find the time to help the leader adjust to their new role.

It may well, in the end, be necessary to find a way of reporting the matter back up the system if the team leader is entrenched and resistant to change, depending on what rule of confidentiality has been agreed, or if it is his/her manager who is at fault. If the fault cannot be tackled within the team, then it is necessary to involve those who have the power to initiate change. Another way of doing this is to set up a further team day and ask the team to invite the appropriate manager to come, so that they can see for themselves what the issues are.

(E) USING SOCIODRAMA

Here a team takes a hypothetical scenario created from a situation that confronts them, such as a difficult client or a future planned management change for their section, and develops this through role play and drama.

Examples of sociodrama are:

o a tenants group exploring relationships between themselves and other tenants on their estate

o senior staff examining ways of managing change in their organisation

o creating typical scenes between men and women to look at gender issues within a team

o looking at how the team tackles a typical, but made up, work situation.

Dramatic situations like these give the team the opportunity to look at how they work, the roles they play in the team, where the blocks are and how these can be changed.

Within the sociodrama the doctor as the director can help move the action on by getting people to double (where people stand beside a person in role and speak as if they are them), and role reverse (where two people who might have a communication difficulty swap roles and take on the role the other person was playing).

Role reversal is particularly helpful in enabling people to understand both how the world looks from another's viewpoint and what they might be contributing to a problematical relationship, by dumping parts of themselves onto the other person.

Doubling helps a person in the role as well as the team to better understand all the different things that might be going on for the individual in that position. Doubling is also, as we saw in sculpting, very useful in bringing out hidden agendas within the team. If the doctor feels that there are things going on in the team which are not being said, then s/he can ask people to say for others what they might be finding difficult to say. On many occasions it will be the doctor who might well have the insight, and also the freedom, in the group to do the doubling. If things that need to be said are not being said, then there are unspoken rules to protect this situation. The team might, for example, feel that if a suspected affair between two members is actually spoken about, then the feelings unleashed will destroy the team. In this case the doctor might want to take this further by doubling or by simply reflecting back to the group how he or she is feeling. For example, 'In this group I am feeling it is unsafe to speak. This makes it difficult to know how to act and I just want to be out of here.' Often someone being prepared to talk like this will give permission for others in the group to share how they are feeling. If the doctor has got it right then the others will echo what s/he has shared and the group is then in a better position to judge whether it is prepared to stay with this feeling or whether it wishes to confront the hidden issue.

If the doctor senses that the group is ready to move on then s/he can play the role of the naive outsider and ask, 'Who in this group has permission to tell me what is happening?'

Again, the content and the process are equally important. It is necessary for the team not only to work through this conflict but to learn from it, so that it can handle ones that occur in the future. For this to happen it is necessary to understand the different roles that people play within groups, which is one of the aims of sociodrama.

Therefore, in a sociodrama the consultant is using the action to help the group explore a situation. It can aid both with diagnosis and, more importantly, with moving the team on as people get an opportunity to explore one another's roles and attitudes. This enables new behaviours to develop and to be practised and for new understandings to emerge.

(F) EXPANDING ROLES

A different way of exploring roles is to ask the whole team to list all the roles that they think team members have ever played, both positive and negative. These are then put onto sheets of paper, turned over and handed out to people in the team. People are then asked to hand their sheet(s) with the different roles on them to the member of the team they think it best fits. People then sit in a circle and look at the roles they have been given, saying how they feel about them. They then move on to discuss the implication of the roles on the team's performance. This helps team members to become aware of how others see them and of how they can change their behaviour where necessary. This exercise can be stressful and needs to be done in a team where there is a good level of trust.

In one team, people were asked to list all the roles that they had experienced other people in the team playing. Each person then clustered the roles they had been given and the facilitator asked each person to give each cluster a family role. A scene was then enacted, with people playing these roles which enabled some long-standing issues to be resolved.

(G) IMPROVING A TEAM'S COMMUNICATION

Another way of looking at communication strategies is to use different coloured balls of string to represent different types of communication within a team (e.g. those about supervision of work, those about support, those about case discussions etc.)

The team puts chairs around the room, one chair for each team member, with a sign to indicate whose chair it is. The group is divided up with each sub-group being given a ball of string and asked to thread it between the chairs to indicate how they see communication flowing within the team. The team can then discuss the different patterns to see whether they all agree, what problems arise because of these patterns, who is at the centre and who is peripheral, how these people and the team as a whole feel about this and what changes they would like to make. The strings can then be rethreaded to show the system that the team wants to have in place.

(H) PAIRED WORK

A useful way of helping events to move forward is to get each team member to spend time with every other team member in turn. This is because some of the difficulties in the team are likely to be because of problems between individuals, which they will not necessarily want to discuss in front of the whole team. I often ask each person in their pairs to finish off the three following sentences:

> 'One thing I like about working with you is…'

> 'One thing that gets in the way of us working well together is…'

> 'In the future I would like us to…'

In very busy teams this might be the only time that some people have said anything significant to each other for months. In these cases the exercise functions primarily as group building.

(I) DEALING WITH ANGER

Sometimes it is clear that people within a team are angry with each other. This anger needs to be expressed in a constructive way. People within a work team, as against a therapy group, have to continue working together the next day delivering a service.

If the doctor feels that the anger is taking the form of projection (i.e. the person is displacing an anger they feel about themselves onto someone else), then the person can be asked to own their feelings by making 'I' statements. This serves two functions. First, it helps the person get in touch with their feelings and, second, it creates space for the other person to respond. In contrast, accusatory 'you' statements produce a defensive reaction which impedes resolution.

A different version of this exercise is to ask the person to make a statement in the form of:

> 'I see… (a description of the behaviour which makes them angry).'

> As a result of this, 'I feel…'

'What I want from you is...'

'And in the meantime I will do...to protect myself.'

An alternative way is to use an empty chair. The person talks to a chair, which can represent a named or unnamed person in the team. This is particularly useful for where the facilitator has a hunch that the real target of the anger lies elsewhere. The facilitator can then ask, 'Who is really in that chair for you?'

Anger between two people in a team can also be a conduit for all the unexpressed anger in the group. Where this is happening the doctor can ask, 'Who else feels like this?' Alternatively two chairs could be set up, reflecting a division in the team, and participants could be asked to double either chair, expressing their feelings towards the other side.

Another way of dealing with the group context is to ask the group, after an angry interchange, how they feel about what they have heard. This puts the ownership for what is happening between the two people back to the group to own and tackle.

A further approach is, as described before, to sculpt the team as a family because people often find it easier to both be angry and to be on the receiving end when they are playing a role.

(J) TRAUMATISED TEAMS

Some staff teams exist in a traumatised state. This might be as a result of a death, a physical attack by a customer, a long-standing split, an aggressive staff member or having a dominant and abusive team leader.

Teams in this situation will often experience a lack of trust, scapegoating, splitting into sub-groups and a culture of blame. The stages the team might go through include denial, anger, depression, acceptance and moving on. In other words, teams react to trauma in a similar way that individuals do to a bereavement.

The task of the doctor is to help the team move through the stages. Often this will be the first time that the team has collectively had an opportunity to tell their story, and the doctor's task is to listen to what has happened and to acknowledge how hard it has been for them. Moving on is sometimes made more difficult by different team members being at varying stages in dealing with the trauma. As a result, it is not unusual in teams like this for one outcome of the intervention being to free some people to leave the team.

(K) DISCUSSION

All of the above are techniques that the doctor can use to help a team examine a problem and come up with new ways to improve team functioning. The crucial point is that, by the end, the doctor has had to find a way of giving ownership of the day back to the team. This can be done, for example, by getting the team, under the direction of the leader, to produce an action plan to carry through any of the conclusions from the day.

Very few people would expect a family therapist to be able to turn around a stuck family in only one or two sessions, but this is often the expectation of a team away day. Therefore, it can only happen if the team are committed to continue working along any new directions when they are back in their workplace.

4. Conclusion

Staff teams are the way in which most organisations work to achieve their tasks. From the individual's viewpoint, teams are the place where their work, social and emotional needs are met.

The importance of teams in industry is being recognised, for example, by the growth of quality circles and the break-up of assembly lines into smaller working units.

In the public sector, particularly in the caring field, teams have been the basic way of organising work. The failure to get the team right in meeting both work and emotional needs can be seen in the high toll that stress takes.

This part is a guide to helping teams perform better. It has looked both at how they come into being and what can be done when they go wrong.

Bibliography

REFERENCES

Alims-Metcalfe, B. (1993) 'A women's ceiling.' *Health Services Journal* 14 October, 25–27.

Belbin, R. (1981) *Management Teams*. Oxford: Heinemann.

Cabinet Office OMCS (1987) *Understanding Stress: Part One*. London: HMSO.

Peters, T. and Austin, N. (1986) *A Passion for Excellence*. Glasgow: Fontana/Collins.

FURTHER READING

Benson, J. (1987) *Working More Creatively with Groups*. London: Tavistock.

Collins, T. and Bruce, T. (1984) *Staff Support and Staff Training*. London: Tavistock.

Douglas, I. (1991) *A Handbook of Common Groupwork Problems*. London: Routledge.

Handy, C. (1987) *Understanding Organisations*. London: Penguin.

Morrison, T., Davies, M., Waters, J., Dale, P. and Roberts, W. (1985) *Surviving in Teams is Not Always Easy*. Rochdale: NSPCC.

Ovretveit, J. (1985) *Organisation of Multi-disciplinary Community Teams*. Brunel: Institute of Organisation and Social Studies.

Payne, M. (1982) *Working in Teams*. London: Macmillan.

Foreword

Sociodrama arose from the upheaval and horror of World War I. It is still being developed by people across the world, but its founder was a young doctor called Jacob Moreno. He lived in Vienna and worked in refugee camps and a children's hospital. In the evenings he helped the city's prostitutes organise for their own protection.

Moreno wanted science to enhance and enrich our humanity. He believed that science must become a tool for the world's convalescence. Battling with the social conflicts, he saw with a clarity, unusual in such a young person, the value of the middle position. Out of it all came a set of ideas for a 'third way' which he called psychodrama. The word was an umbrella term coined to represent his philosophy, his methodologies and his techniques, all action-based. He designed the techniques to give life to the philosophy. The energy source for these methods is each person's potential to be spontaneous and creative.

In this current historical period of categorising and specialisation, the word psychodrama is used widely to describe Moreno's method of group therapy. The method uses drama to help people come to terms with or solve personal problems. The aim is therapy, education and change, both in and beyond the clinic.

Sociodrama is different. The subject is the group. The theme is an agreed group problem. The aim is education plus action for creative social change beyond the classroom. Both methods attempt to sow the seeds of change. Psychodrama looks at the roots of a problem, while sociodrama looks at the soil in which our collective roots are formed or deformed. Sociodrama treats the sickness of society that in turn makes its members ill. There has never been a better time for treatment.

Ken Sprague
Holwell '95
International Centre for
Psychodrama and Sociodrama

1. Introduction

1.1 TARGET AUDIENCE

This part is aimed at three different groups of people:

(a) trainers who run and facilitate groups in areas such as management of change, team building, dealing with stress etc

(b) group leaders who work with groups exploring social issues such as the environment. These might be youth club workers, teachers, community leaders, probation staff etc

(c) people with a background in psychodrama who wish to develop their skills in using sociodrama.

This is very much a 'how-to-do' guide for practitioners. There is a further reading list at the back for those who want to delve more deeply.

1.2 WHAT IS SOCIODRAMA?

Sociodrama is a social learning activity based in a group setting. Participants explore a subject which reflects the interests of group members. This can range from developing assertive skills in a social skills group to tackling racial differences in a community. Moreno (1993, p.89) saw sociodramatists as having:

> the task to organise preventive, didactic and reconstruction meetings in the community in which they live and work; to organise, upon call, such meetings in problem areas everywhere; to enter communities confronted with emergent or chronic social issues, to enter mass meetings of strikes, race riots, rallies of political parties, and so forth, and to handle and clarify the situation on the spot.

Kellerman (1996) similarly talks of three applications of sociodrama: first, in tackling traumatic events and social crises such as in critical incident debriefs; second, in times of political change and social disintegration such as work with community organisations opposing redevelopment; and, third, in areas of social diversity such as confronting racism.

The emphasis in this section will be on the use of sociodramatic techniques in small group situations, although some examples of other uses are given at the end.

A sociodrama has three primary aims:

o   an improved understanding of a social situation

o   an increase in participants' knowledge about their own and other people's roles in relation to that situation

o   an emotional release or catharsis as people express their feelings about the subject.

Therefore, in a group of industrial training consultants, for example, the common theme that emerged was working with organisational change. The session enabled participants to explore the different forces aiding or impeding change and the ways they could intervene, as well as giving voice to the feelings they had experienced when facilitating workshops in this area.

As was discussed in the foreword, sociodrama is closely related to psychodrama as a technique. There are, however, important differences. A psychodrama is a therapeutic event, also taking place in a group setting, but where the focus is on one individual, the protagonist, whose therapeutic issue is being explored.

For example, if the subject was loneliness, in a psychodrama the protagonist would explore where that feeling came from and how it was affecting their present emotional state. In a sociodrama the group would create a hypothetical scene to look at how and why people came to feel lonely and what could be done about it.

A further difference is that psychodramas are based on real events that have happened to people (though imaginary events might well become part of the action), while sociodramas generally use scenes that are made up, though they will have links to real events that have happened to participants.

Sociodrama also has close links to role play. The main difference is that role play is usually a short scene, enacted with the prime focus of learning new skills or developing an understanding of different roles. Though these might also be some of the aims of a sociodrama, in the latter the action will flow through a number of scenes, a greater variety of techniques will be used and the learning might include not only skills and role learning but also a historical, economic and/or social understanding of the themes being explored.

It could be argued that the same effect could be achieved by a lecture. Sociodrama, in contrast, is an action-orientated method which believes that people learn best if they can be involved in exploring issues from a variety of perspectives engaging both thoughts and feelings.

Another related technique, which is used to look at issues of oppression is Boal's forum theatre (Boal 1992), where members of the group or audience come on stage and work on situations in which people have found themselves to be disempowered, to explore alternative ways of tackling them.

1.3 HISTORY

While the use of drama as a creative way of informing, involving and educating people about the world is as old as drama itself, the specific techniques used in sociodrama stem from the works of Moreno as described in the foreword, who is better known as the founder of psychodrama.

Even though Moreno was concerned with both the health of the individual and the cosmos as a whole, psychodrama has become far better known as a methodology than sociodrama. This might well be because changing the individual is always, in societal terms, a safer and more respectable approach and less challenging to the existing power order than one based on getting groups of people to examine issues in a collective manner.

1.4 USES

The prime uses of sociodramas as a training tool are:

(1) as a training tool in, for example, work with staff working with older people

(2) in learning more about roles, such as trainee travel couriers gaining a better understanding of how typical package tour 'disaster scenarios' develop and the options which exist for defusing them

(3) as part of a team-building process

(4) in connection with discovering more about social issues such as HIV/AIDS

(5) as a way of looking at roles and issues within groups.

These will be explored in more detail later in the section.

1.5 TECHNIQUES

The basic techniques used in sociodrama are:

(1) doubling the individual and the group

(2) sculpting

(3) role reversal

(4) soliloquy

(5) role plays.

These will be discussed in more detail later.

1.6 ROLES

Working with roles is a core part of a sociodramatist's work. A role is an identification of a significant aspect of human functioning. Roles can be:

o social, for example teacher;

o individualistic, for example self-doubter or psychosomatic.

In psychodrama, role theory is used to help develop a person's interpersonal functioning (Clayton 1993). Here, roles might be classified as progressive, dysfunctional or coping, and the psychodramatist's work would be concerned with increasing the effectiveness of human relationships.

In sociodrama, we are concerned primarily with social roles. This might be in terms of helping people to understand roles, in terms of their different elements – actions, feelings and values – and where conflicts might arise. Therefore, for doctors, there might be intra-role conflict between expectations of being the scientist and also the empathic teller of bad news, and inter-role conflict between the caring professional and the hard-headed fund-holder.

In many conflict situations, sociodramatists will be concerned to help people understand the world from other people's roles; swapping gender roles would be an obvious example. In a community setting it might be useful for activists to understand the constraints under which a housing manager operates. However, that understanding might be deterimental in so far as it might make a group more reluctant to act; it is not always politically helpful to see both sides of the coin. A sociodramatist operating in the wider community needs to be clear about the political dimensions and how this ties in with her/his own set of values.

It is also useful to understand how roles operate within groups. Therefore in one 'stuck' group its life history was recreated from conception to the present, with people using the scenes to explore the roles they had played.

2. The Stages of a Sociodrama

2.1 PLANNING

In a sociodrama the workshop is led by a director. The director ensures that the session achieves its aims in a safe and creative manner. The director will need a background in working with groups and some training in group work, creative training techniques, counselling or psycho-/sociodrama.

The director has to bear a number of points in mind. The first is to be aware of the type of group s/he is being asked to work with. There are two basic groups in this context. First, there are those set up specifically to use sociodrama as a method to explore internal or external group issues. Second, there are those groups who meet for another task, such as a training group on managing change, where sociodrama might turn out to be an appropriate tool. Whether it is appropriate or not will depend on:

- o the culture of the group. Some groups give out the message, 'we are not here to play'

- o the learning outcomes (i.e. what has been agreed to be achieved by the end of the session). A very task-focused group is likely to see a sociodrama excursion as an irrelevance

- o the length of time. A successful sociodrama requires enough time to create a safe working atmosphere

- o the skill of the director. Directors need to feel confident that they can deal appropriately with whatever issues surface if they go down the sociodramatic route

- o the contract between the director and the group. The original contract negotiated at the beginning of the day might have specified learning methods. If they did not involve experiential learning, then this might need to be re-negotiated

o the setting in which the session is taking place. Some rooms are simply not large or physically safe enough for sociodrama. This depends, in part, on the size of the group.

A second point involves issues to do with power or anti-discriminatory practice. This will cover a number of different areas:

o the room in which the action is taking place. Is it, for example, accessible for wheelchair users?

o the director's background. If white, male, middle-class and heterosexual, then what biases might stem from this in his perception of what is going on for group members, his use of language, and also how people from different backgrounds might perceive him?

o an awareness of the group membership and how it might feel for people from less powerful societal groups. If there is one black person in a group of white people, or one female in a group of males, how does one make it safe for them and find a way of empowering their membership and group involvement?

A third point is that the room needs to be large enough to create one or more scenes. It will need to be private enough so that participants feel that they are not overlooked or overheard. It also needs to be physically safe so there is little risk of bodily harm. Ideally, it will have a range of furniture to help scene setting and to provide a variety of atmospheres for different stages of the action.

A fourth point is that the director needs to prepare him/herself for the day. This will involve finding out about the group and contemplating various ways of starting the day and how the action might proceed. If the subject matter is clear, then the director will have to do some research. Even though group members are likely to have a lot of knowledge about the area, the director must be prepared to fill in gaps. S/he will also need the information to help guide the action, remembering that a sociodrama will involve some social learning. Finally, the director must prepare him/herself. The main part of directing a sociodrama comes from being able to 'hear' the group at work. This means that the director is able to listen to both what is said and what is inferred by people's words and actions so that s/he can identify themes and issues. In order for this to happen the director must have space within him/her self to be able to notice and feel what is happening in the group.

2.2 THE WARM-UP

The first stage of a sociodrama is the warm-up. This consists of many different parts:

1. *The director's warm-up*

Following on from above, unless the director is ready to work, then s/he will have difficulty in making the group function. The director's warm-up involves a number of aspects:

- getting the feel of the room. How should the furniture be arranged? Where is a good space to set the action?

- sorting out the bureaucratic details, such as tea/coffee provision for the day

- focusing on the day and what might happen. As the aim is to work around a group theme, it is wrong for the directors to impose a theme on the group. If they do, they are likely to experience resistance and a lack of energy with which to work. The exception to this is where the workshop has been advertised as being about a particular topic.

- developing their own spontaneity. Part of the thrust of a sociodramatic enaction is participants creating scenes and roles. This involves participants being spontaneous. But it also places an equal need on the director to be creative, especially in a group unused to a sociodramatic way of working. While this is, in part, an essential lifeskill for a director – working with children is good practice – it is necessary before each session for the director to feel energised and alive.

2. *The group warm-up*

This has many different parts:

(a) Creating a group. Unless it is an ongoing group, at the start the director will be faced with a number of individuals, some of whom might know each other, with a varying degree of knowledge about sociodrama. One of the first tasks is to turn the individuals into a group. This could be done through a variety of exercises:

- asking people to place themselves in the room in terms of how far they have travelled to get to the course on the day, where they were born etc.

- getting people to say whom they know in the group and how that makes them feel
- putting people into groups of three or four and getting them to find four or five non-obvious things that they have in common
- naming games, such as throwing a ball of wool to someone and calling out their name at the same time. The aim is to build links between people
- using story telling, perhaps getting people to tell a tale of how they came to be here today. Alternatively, it could be a sequential story, each person, in turn, adding something.

(b) Warming people up to the room. If the session is to work, then people need to own the room and feel comfortable in all parts of it. It is therefore useful to do an exercise which moves people around the space:

- asking people to see who can be first to touch all the sides of the room
- getting people to walk around the room and find a part they feel most/least at home in and getting them to share that feeling and the reasons for it with the person/s nearest to them

Both these exercises need to take into account any physical disabilities group members might have and the suitability of the room.

(c) Building safety. Unless people feel safe with the group, the director and the room, they are unlikely to take risks in the sharing or in the enactment. Making people feel safe can be done in a number of ways:

- by the director's introduction, which needs to show his/her competence
- by welcoming the group members and giving them a structure for the day
- by getting everyone to introduce themselves. This is both an act of joining and an opportunity for the director to listen to what is happening for individuals
- by giving people an opportunity to share how it feels being there

- by setting up some group rules. The most important are likely to be rules about confidentiality, respect and power. Unless people feel that whatever happens will remain confidential to the group, they are unlikely to share much about themselves. Respect for what people say and how they say it is important so that people will feel confident they will be listened to. Issues to do with power concern the power that participants possess, either through force of character or as representatives of powerful groups in society. It is important that they don't exercise that power in a way that re-creates within the group power differences within the wider society. There will, of course, be scenarios when these power differences are the main theme the group works on, but the director still needs to find a way of working on them which empowers people. Therefore low-status staff in an organisation might have the opportunity to take on the role of a trade union negotiator.

(d) Physically warming people up. If there is little energy then the group might need to be energised by physical exercises. These might include:

- moving parts of the body
- moving around the room in different ways; for example, assertively, aggressively and submissively
- exercises in pairs, for example one person with eyes shut being led around the room by their partner by touch or sound
- exercises in small groups, for example getting people to position their bodies so that they create a machine such as a car engine and having the machine move with appropriate sounds.

(e) An acting warm-up. Since sociodrama involves an element of acting, the group might need a relevant warm-up to get over the fear that some people might have of doing something silly. Possible exercises include:

- people standing in a circle; the director then asks two people to walk across the group and meet each other as, for example, long-lost school friends, secret lovers, teacher and pupil etc.

- an object being passed around with people having to mime another object it could become, for example a ruler being used as a pen or as a comb.

Unless the warm-up is done well, the rest of the session won't work. Time spent in warm-up is rarely wasted.

Once this stage of the warm-up is finished, then the main part of the warm-up can begin.

2.3 FIND THE GROUP THEME

After the group warm-up, the director's task is to help the group find the theme or issue that it is going to work on. This won't always be necessary if the group has come to work together on a previously agreed or advertised topic.

However, even then, it might still be necessary to find the particular aspect that the group wants to look at.

There are a number of ways of doing this:

○ By talking. The director asks the people to move into groups of two or three and to talk about what issues are current for them or what has brought them to the course on the day. These may then be shared with the group as a whole, or each small group may meet up with another to see if they can agree on a theme. If there are a number of possibilities, the director can then help the group make a sociometric choice (i.e. the group chooses by its actions). In this case the director could designate three different parts of the room, each to represent a possible topic, and then ask people to move to the part which reflects the issue they most want to tackle. The issue chosen by most people would be the one the group would then work on.

○ By using photos. The director lays out a number of photos of people (making sure that they are representative of the racial, ethnic, gender, class and disability mix in society) with varying expressions and in different situations and asks group members to choose the photo they most/least associate with.

○ With newspapers. The director asks people to read through a selection of papers and find a story which somehow grabs their attention. In both of these, some form of sociometric choice will then have to be made (i.e. group members move to the photo or story with which they most strongly identify). The item with the most votes is the one chosen.

- By asking people to choose an object – a piece of clothing, something in their handbag or wallet or something lying around the room which has some significance for them. Out of this sharing, a theme, such as 'loneliness' or 'stuck in a relationship', is likely to emerge.

- With balls of wool. The director asks people to bring along different coloured balls of wool and then to weave them between each other, creating a pattern that reflects how each group member is feeling. Again, there then needs to be a sharing to label the group feeling/theme.

- By sellotaping together a number of flipchart sheets of paper and then asking people to draw something which reflects what they are thinking or feeling. The director then gets the group to look at the drawings and, working together, find a common focus. Alternatively, people can be asked to brainstorm on the paper all the themes that are around for them and then group them until a central concern emerges.

2.4 SETTING THE SCENE

Once the theme has been identified it needs to be given a focus, a scene in which the various parts of it can be explored. The scene can suggest itself from the previous discussion in identifying the theme; it can come from one or more of the group members or it can come from the director.

Once identified, the scene needs to be given a physical presence. Let us suppose we are dealing with child abuse as the theme and the scene is a family meeting. The questions that need to be asked are:

- what type of family?

- what type of meeting? At meal time? While watching TV?

- in which room is it taking place? What is in this room (furniture, decorations etc.)?

- who is in the room?

- who else is in the family? Who could enter the scene? Here the aim is to identify possible roles that people can take as the action develops;

- what other roles might be relevant (neighbour, teacher etc.)?

The first step is then to build the room and give it a character. All the group members, if possible, should be involved in this so as to help them become identified with it. One way of giving the room and its occupants some historical identity is to get group members to role reverse with one of the objects (e.g. to become a grandfather clock and, speaking as the clock, talk about what they have seen happen in the room).

The next step is then to create the roles of the family members. People volunteer to take different roles (e.g. father, mother, daughter, grandmother). In order to help them to become that person, it is useful if the director questions them.

DIRECTOR: 'Tell us something about yourself and you family.'

MOTHER: 'I am 42, my name is Helen. This is not always a happy family. My husband and I don't have much to say to each other any more.'

If the person playing Mother had replied using 'she' instead of 'I' it would have been a sign to the director that s/he had not yet taken on the role.

People playing new roles will often play them in a stereotypical manner (i.e. exaggerating the perceived essential aspects – for example, playing a Jewish mother as interfering and over-protective). As the action develops, role playing becomes typical of how people actually behave. This comes about as the person identifies with the role and puts his/her own understanding into it. Finally, the role sometimes gets played as an archetype, that is it captures the universal aspect of a role. In the case of a mother, it could be those behaviours which encompass the idea of the 'earth mother'. When this occurs, strong identifications take place in the group as there is something evoked for all participants in terms of their relationships to their own mothers.

2.5 STRUCTURING THE ACTION

Before going on to look at the action phase, we need to consider the way things can be structured in a sociodrama.

Sociodrama is a creative group activity in that, when a scene starts, it can develop its own momentum from the way the actors play the existing roles and create new ones. There has to be some structure, however, if chaos is not to ensue.

The director has an important role to play here. S/he has to indicate:

o when people can join in

o which part of the action is highlighted and where the rest need to pause.

One way of doing this is by the director using her/his fist as a mike dangling over the group members the director wishes to focus on. This choice will be determined by the logic of the scene and the learning potential of different aspects of the plot.

Another part of the structure is to have somewhere for people to go if they don't see a role for themselves at the moment. Depending on the room or the action, there can either be a 'non-action space' or a safe wall where people can shed a role and become available for another one.

Once people take a role, what happens if they want to move on and try a different role? Sometimes, of course, the role is only a minor player in the scene and it does not matter if it disappears. On other occasions, it might be central to the plot, for example the role of the change agent in a sociodrama about organisational development. In cases like this, the role can be held by a chair, so that whoever sits on an identified chair becomes the change agent, or by a part of the stage. For example, in a sociodrama which involved different parts of the body talking to one another, there was a space for the head, heart, stomach and genitals, and more than one person could occupy the space at one time.

In a sociodrama, we are concerned both with what is said and also what is thought or felt. This can be expressed by doubling. There needs, therefore, to be a way for people to indicate when they are doubling. If roles are held by people sitting in chairs, then doubling could be indicated by people standing behind the relevant chair. If people in roles are standing and moving about, then doubling can be indicated by putting a hand on the shoulder.

2.6 THE ACTION

The scene starts. In terms of what happens next, there are different things to consider:

1. The role of the director

As we saw in the previous section, one of the functions of the director is to decide which part of the action to highlight.

A second task is to keep an eye on the flow of the action. S/he has to decide:

- when has the scene finished

- where could it go to next

- what scene should follow.

In making these decisions, the director will need to keep in mind the learning taking place, the flow of energy and the logic of the action.

Another task for the director is keeping an eye on all the participants to see:

o who looks as though they would like to join in (has an 'act hunger') but cannot see a way in

o who looks like they might be distressed by what they are experiencing

o who is stuck in a role and cannot get out of it

o who might obtain a useful insight by taking on another role.

In these cases the director needs to note what is happening and then decide how to deal with it. S/he might:

o pause the action and allow a particular individual time to say what is happening to him/her

o quietly suggest a role

o actively indicate a role reversal. A particular time this might be necessary is when the director can see that, while playing a role, someone is being triggered by past memories. As the contract is for sociodrama rather than psychodrama, the director needs to move the person out of the role. This gives the person the opportunity to observe what is happening rather than being overwhelmed by it. The triggering, however, might indicate that this is an important role for the group and this is why role reversal is a useful technique as someone else can be swapped into it.

2. Energy

For a scene to work, it needs energy. What happens if there is no energy or if the energy disappears? If there is no energy at the start, then it is likely that:

o the warm-up was inadequate and the group had not jelled properly

o the theme chosen did not reflect the real issue the group as a whole wanted to address

o the scene did not allow the feelings in the theme to be expressed

o people had not engaged with the roles

o the roles in the scene were too limited.

If the energy goes from a scene once it has started, then it might be because:

- the scene is finished. There is nothing more to say

- the scene is too powerful. The lack of energy is a defensive measure against strong feelings. This may also be a reflection on the lack of safety in the group

- the scene has taken a direction which is only owned by one or two group members.

The choices open to the director are to:

- trust his/her intuition as to the cause of the lack of energy and as to what to do next

- reflect the situation back to the group and allow the discussion to lead to the next action. It is like pressing a pause button on the video. It might well be that the issue for the group is not some external scene but is to do with dynamics in the group; the next scene will have to find a way of dealing with that. It might, for example, start with the group differences being given a geographical space in the room, then allowing some of the voices that go with the spaces to be heard. It is then necessary to find a scene where these sorts of voices can be found, that is moving from a particular scene in the group to a general scene so as to explore what is universal in the group; then, in the closing, to bring it back to the group.

This is one dynamic a sociodrama can take – to move from a particular scene and to find a way of understanding it by broadening the canvas and then bringing it back, with any new insights gained, to the original scene. In this way a sociodrama can have the same circularity that a psychodrama has, where it moves from a problem scene in the present life of the protagonist back to an earlier life scene from where the existing difficulty stemmed. Once there has been some resolving of the difficulty, the action reverts to the original scene, with an opportunity to tackle the problem there with a fresh approach. This flow is part of the internal logic to which the socio-drama director has to pay attention in determining the flow of the action.

3. *Difficult roles*

There are many difficult roles that people play. Two, in particular, that directors need to be aware of are the abhorrent role and the alien role.

The abhorrent role is that of an 'evil' person, such as a racist in a sociodrama about oppression. It is often an essential role but one that people don't want to fill. Sociodrama relies more on people volunteering to take on roles, while in a psychodrama the protagonist will ask people to play roles. The director, therefore, has to make the role safe. S/he also has to be aware of the need to double-de-role, the person playing the role at the end of the session; that is, they need to be de-roled so that they themselves separate from the role, but they also need to be separated from the role in the eyes of the rest of the group.

One way of handling roles such as these is to have them held by a chair, with people free to come and sit briefly while making a statement and then moving on. This enables a number of people to feel safer in seeing what the world looks like from this perspective.

A different difficult role is where someone is playing a role alien to them: men playing women, for example, or white people playing black people. It is important for people to enact these roles, as one of the aims of sociodrama is to give people an understanding of other people's roles and to broaden their view of social issues.

The need is to play the role with respect while recognising that initial portrayers are likely to start at a stereotypical level. In this case, roles can be built on with the director helping the person by asking them relevant questions, by group members doubling the person in the role and by group discussion and role reversal.

2.7 TECHNIQUES

A specific part of the action is the techniques available to the director to move the action on. These include:

(1) Sculpting

This is using people or objects to build a picture which shows the underlying dynamic of a situation. It can be useful in a training group as a safe way of warming people up to taking on a more active role. In a sculpt there is no need for people to have to take on a speaking part. If, for example, the theme was family dynamics, the director could start by getting the group to create a hypothetical family. This might turn out to be stereotypical – a mother, a father and two children. The director could then ask people to volunteer for different roles. Subsequently, the director would request the group to come up with ideas as to the possible dynamics between the family members. These could then be sculpted so that people could see the dynamics; the physical positions, the spaces between them and the postures the characters took would represent the relationships between them.

Therefore, how the mother and father are physically placed together will indicate how they are perceived to relate. Arm in arm, looking at each other, would imply a close, double bed, intimate relationship. Back to back might imply separate beds with communication difficulties. Similarly the posture they held would also carry a message about them – for example a stiff pose with a pointing finger would suggest an authoritarian personality.

Similarly, with the children, where they were placed would indicate which parent they related to most. How they looked at the parent and how they held themselves would indicate the nature of this relationship.

If s/he wanted to move the sculpt, the director could get the group to double each position and/or let the people holding the roles begin speaking. At this point it would be moving from a sculpt into sociodramatic action.

The director can also take participants out of the sculpt and let them view it. This is akin to some of Boal's (1995) work. This is very useful when a person in a sculpt feels strongly about the situation. Stepping out gives him/her space to reflect on this and perhaps to change the sculpt in a way that is meaningful to her/him.

It is important that group members have the opportunity to comment on the process of building the sculpt, as this often stirs up memories and feelings.

It is also possible to use sculpting at the stage of finding a group theme. The director could ask people to move so that the spaces between them and the position held indicated the relationships that existed in the group. The director could then get participants to name the relationships and choose which one people wanted to work on.

A further way of sculpting is to use objects. This, too, can be done as part of the process of finding a topic to work on. The director could say: 'Find objects in the room which represent you and people in your present/birth family and build a sculpt with them.' After this, people could walk around and look for common themes between all the sculpts.

(2) Doubling

As we have seen, doubling is where a group member puts him/herself beside a person in a role and gives voice to that person's unspoken thoughts and feelings. The more the doubler mimics the posture and actions of the person they are doubling, the easier it is to do.

Doubling can be used in a number of ways. It can be used, as indicated above, to expand a role by expressing the unsaid aspects of an interaction:

HUSBAND (TO WIFE):   'I'm tired.'

HUSBAND'S DOUBLE: 'I'm angry with you, you don't realise how hard I work and the crap I have to put up with all day.'

A second way is where someone in the group might see that there is something else the character could say in the interaction rather than simply thinking it:

| HUSBAND: | 'I'm tired.' |
| DOUBLE: | 'I'm tired of this conversation.' |

A third way is where the double is used to give support to a person in a role. A person holding a role, for example that of someone with HIV, might want to stay with it but either might be blocked or begin to feel distressed. In this case a double, coming alongside and holding the same body posture to maximise empathic understanding, can lend support, sometimes by speaking and sometimes just by their presence.

The director may have people as permanent doubles for as long as the role lasts; group members may come up, double, then move back out of the action; alternatively, people may start as doubles then either take over the role or share it. The choice will be dependent on the learning to be gained for the individuals concerned and the group as a whole.

Similarly, the director will sometimes need to indicate when the person holding the role should speak and when the double should speak. Too many doubling interventions can stem the flow of the scene but, on other occasions, what the double(s) have to say might be the most important thing.

(3) Voices

A particular form of sociodramatic doubling is that of 'voices'. In any scene there will be any number of different perspectives. Therefore in a scene about family life, 'voices' might include:

o the women's movement

o church

o sanctity of the family

o government ministers

o older person viewing historical changes

o a woman not wanting children

o an unreconstituted male.

Sometimes there may be appropriate roles to express these voices or they may come in, as a double. Sometimes, however, they are voices heard offstage in real life but they create the wider perspective within which the scene is taking place. Encouraging people to be a 'voice' is therefore one way of building in this societal viewpoint. It also means the director must always be encouraging people to be 'warmed up', to look for a way to contribute and develop the action. Simply keeping group members on their feet helps with the energy. It is also why sociodrama is a group action learning method par excellence: there is always a way in which participants can engage.

(4) Role reversal

Role reversal, as the name implies, is where a person moves out of one role and into another.

It is most often used when a person in a role is in some form of confrontation with another and it is important for the person to get an understanding of how the situation looks from another perspective.

For example:

WOMAN: 'Typical of a man, you never have anything to say when it comes down to it.'

DIRECTOR: 'Role reversal.'

MAN AS WOMAN   REPEATS LAST WORDS:
                '…you never have anything to say when it comes down to it.'

WOMAN AS MAN:
                'That's because…'

It is also useful when answering questions:

WOMAN: 'I don't have a clue what men think about that.'

DIRECTOR: 'Role reversal.'

In sociodrama, it can also be used to put people into a role where the director feels they have something important to say.

GROUP MEMBER: 'If I were you…'

DIRECTOR: 'Become her – reverse roles.'

In addition it can be used, as we have seen, to take people out of roles when they need protection.

(5) Soliloquy

This is where the director gives a person space, while in the role, to say whatever is going on for them. It might be important for the person to explore the role in a way which the present action in the scene does not enable them to.

2.8 ENDINGS

As we have seen, there is often a circularity to a sociodrama – it starts with a scene, moves out to broader issues, then comes back and gives fresh insight to the first scene and the theme it represents. Sometimes the logic of the plot will lead down a different path. There is a risk of trying to create happy endings – arms linked in a collective struggle routing the manifestation of evil. While one theme of a sociodrama is to explore possible areas of action, there are rarely easy answers. After the end of the action there comes the time for sharing. There are at least four different aspects:

(1) Sharing from role

People share what they learnt from playing different roles. One aim for sociodrama is to build an awareness of roles, to expand people's understanding of them. Their sharing helps to do this. After this happens, participants need to be de-roled, that is, to let go of the thoughts and feelings that belong to the role they were playing. One way of doing this is for people to share with another group member two ways in which they are different from the role they played and one thing they like about themselves.

(2) Sharing out of role

This is where people share what the experience was like for them and what memories are brought up. Another aim for sociodrama is catharsis, or emotional release. This sharing provides space, either to do this or to share where it happened for people during the sociodrama.

(3) Sharing about the theme

This is where people share what they have learnt about the group theme or issue they decided to work on. A further aim of sociodrama is to learn about social situations. This is where this takes place. In doing this it is important to make sure that all viewpoints are respected; otherwise there is a risk that a liberal consensus will predominate and alternative views will be censored.

(4) Sharing about the process

This is particularly important in any training situation. This is where the group and the director reflect on how the sociodrama ran, and what the learning has been for the director and the participants. This will often take place after a break, as it requires people to step outside the process so that they can review what happened. Also, if it happens too soon, it brings to a premature halt some of the cathartic learning.

3. Sociodramas Based on Real Events

As we have seen, classical sociodramas are based on hypothetical scenarios, although these will be based on real events that people have experienced or envisioned. The reasons for this are, first, that if it is based on one individual's event, it will become an individual rather than a group experience. Second, it would be more likely to make it a therapeutic rather than an educational experience. Third, if based on a real situation the action becomes limited to what actually happened in that situation. Fourth, if based on a personal event then the subsequent action becomes influenced at a number of different levels by the needs of the person whose event it is, and it often becomes difficult to disentangle for the other participants and the director.

There are some occasions when a real situation is used as a starting point. There might, for example, be a common experience that most group members share. The point is that the sociodramatic exploration should not be bound by what actually happened, but should enable people to look at the situation from different perspectives and thus gain a new understanding of it.

Another example would be where a participant wanted to examine what was happening in a training group that s/he was facilitating elsewhere. The director would first need to get the approval of the group to work on the issue.

One way of then proceeding would be to re-create the training group, perhaps using sculpting to explore its dynamics. The director could then move the action to a hypothetical group which would enable general characteristics of group behaviour to be explored without being restricted by the known behaviour of the training group members. These insights could then be taken back into the training group and used to examine what might be happening in this group.

A second way would be to set the training group up and then let the person whose group it is explore different ways of running the group. The director here uses the same sociodramatic techniques to help the facilitator practise the role. Role reversal may be used, either to help her see how an intervention by her might be experienced by a group member or to put other group members into the facilitator role, either to help the facilitator see new ways of performing the role or as self-learning for them. In this case the needs of the group, unless the issue is a theme for the whole group, are being subordinated to the needs of one of its individual members.

Another scenario in which a sociodrama might become real is where a group member gets emotionally triggered by the action and the director, with the person and the group's permission, decides to work on what the issue is. This, then, becomes a person-centred sociodrama or a psychodrama happening within a sociodramatic context. The director has the choice of exploring the issue for the protagonist within the confines of the triggering scene, with other group members becoming auxiliaries, that is, playing key roles in that person's life, or moving it on, or back, to the causative scene.

4. Case Examples

The aim here is to show a variety of different settings where either a full-blown sociodrama was run, or where sociodramatic techniques were used to enhance group learning.

4.1 CHILD PROTECTION

This was a workshop for professionals working in the field of child protection. The aim was to explore issues to do with both the causes and the investigation of child abuse. The theme was therefore part of the joining contract.

After a warm-up, a family scene was created (the roles selected by the group – e.g. step-parent, grandparent – carried implicit theories about who was most likely to abuse or be abused). Roles were held by chairs, with rules about doubling and the creation of new roles outlined. The only other brief was that somewhere during the action it had to become clear that abuse was taking, or had taken, place. Each time this has been run, the abuser/survivor pattern has been different. The action finished with the discovery of the abuse. There was time, then, for sharing from and about roles and for learning about theories of abuse, based on the roles selected and how the action unfolded.

After lunch, the groups were given the choice either to follow the case from the professional's or from the family's viewpoint and, depending on their interest, different groups chose different options. In the case of following the professional line through to a case conference, this gave participants the opportunity to explore and learn about one another's roles (i.e. social workers playing police, probationers playing paediatricians, and so on). Here the main learning was about roles.

When the life of the family was followed through to a family re-union some 20 years on, although there was some role learning and some learning about different aspects of abuse, the main learning was cathartic, with people having an opportunity to explore and/or release feelings they held about abuse.

4.2 OLDER PEOPLE

This was a short workshop with a group of people over the age of 75. After a brief warm-up (mainly to introduce the director since the group members knew one another well), the scene setting proceeded via story telling about past times. This led onto the re-creation of a social gathering as it used to happen, including the opportunity to dance. The learning was to do with reminiscence work, remembering and rehearsing old skills.

4.3 WORKERS WITH OLDER PEOPLE

The aim of the workshop was to give people who cared for older people some idea of what it was like to be on the receiving end (see Wiener and Traynor 1987–8). The whole exercise, therefore, was a giant role reversal. People were asked to come as one of the older people for whom they were a key worker. Relevant props were supplied, such as distorting glasses, zimmer frames etc. The scene was a day centre. Even though the roles were based on real characters, because participants came from a number of different centres, the centre for the day itself (which took place in a large training room), as well as the interactions, were hypothetical. People had to stay in role for the whole day. Most commented on how boring life was and came to realise why events such as mealtimes, which broke the day up, were so important.

On another occasion, this exercise was run as the first session of an 18-month 'management of change' exercise, with a departmental management team, both to create a common set of values and to team-build the group.

4.4 A SESSION WITH ORGANISERS OF VOLUNTARY CARERS

The morning session was first spent on warm-up. It was a large group of about 80 people and the main thrust of the warm-up was to get people to interact with as many other people as possible. The second part of the morning was spent on identifying the crucial issues involved in working with volunteers. These included recruitment and training.

After lunch, chairs were placed in a huge circle, with two chairs in the middle. Two people volunteered to sit in these seats and took on the role of voluntary organisers. The rest of the group then became potential volunteers and were asked to give all the reasons they could think of as to why people volunteered or did not. Those who could see positive reasons then moved their seats forward and then the director asked them what their needs from the organisation were. These were listed, and the volunteers were asked if they wished to continue. Most did and they stayed in the centre; the rest moved back to the outer circle.

The action then moved through the stages of the volunteers being trained. When the spotlight turned on to the two organisers, the rest of the group were asked to double their concerns. The reasons for doing this were to make sure all the voices in the group were heard, to encourage group participation and to protect the people in the two key roles from having to do all the work.

The next stage was to put the people in the outer circle into role as people in the community, meeting volunteers and saying what they wanted. This then moved on to an exchange between the different groups (organisers, volunteers and carers) as to who should, and who did, have what say in matching volunteers with carers.

As the session progressed, key points were recorded on flip charts. At the end, people were put into small groups to share their feelings and their learning from the day.

4.5 POLITICS

This was based on a WEA class, looking at what socialism meant in practice. Each week the class became a committee of a post-revolutionary socialist council and then acted out a committee meeting drawing up a programme of action. People were able to try out different perspectives.

4.6 MANAGING CHANGE

The focus was on working with groups wanting to understand and manage change in their organisation. In one session the scene chosen was an ocean voyage, with the group as the crew leaving land (the present structure) on a voyage to a largely unknown foreign shore. This enabled a whole range of issues to be explored: feelings about leaving; what maps were needed; the role of the officers on the ship; what might be the rocks; was there a siren; what was needed for a safe landing etc. The session finished with the crew sending back a message to the main party as to how they should proceed.

In a different workshop, the group built the existing structure at one end of the room and the new structure at the far end. This provided an opportunity to discharge feelings as well as to share knowledge. All the roles that were involved were represented, with people having the opportunity to explore a variety of viewpoints. The action then consisted of moving down the room, step-by-step, looking at what needed to happen, who needed to say what to whom and what the difficulties were.

4.7 LIFE HISTORIES

This was developed for use with fostering and residential workers involved in making difficult placements (see McMillan and Wiener 1988). The scene in this case is based on a real family situation. The participants are all the workers connected with the family and the placement.

There is a story teller, who is the person with the most knowledge about the situation. The action starts as far back in the family history as possible. Participants take on key roles, sitting on the floor as children, kneeling and standing as they grow older. At each crucial stage a scene is enacted between the key roles. Sculpting takes place as children are moved around the room from one placement to another. There is scope for doubling and role reversal.

This method has proved very effective in:

- o building up a picture of the key child's emotional life

- o enabling participants literally to 'see' the child's life unfold in front of them

- o understanding why there have been so many difficulties in placements

- o learning how and why things have gone wrong

- o preparing strategies for dealing with the future

- o creating a common picture for all the workers.

4.8 WORKING WITH TEAMS

The focus was on helping training officers develop group consultancy skills. After a warm-up, the group created an imaginary staff team, with the roles held by different chairs with a piece of paper containing the key characteristics of each role. Each person then had a turn, becoming the consultant to sort out differences in the team; participants were free to 'double' roles. At critical points, all participants were de-roled and then became team consultants in small groups, working out what could happen next.

Another workshop was held as a group supervision exercise. Each person in turn had space to recreate their own staff team, with group members playing the roles. People were put into role, by the person whose team it was, speaking in the first person as they stood behind each chair in turn. Though the scenes were based on real incidents, the role playing enabled the scene to be developed, with the team leader able to try out different ways of tackling problems. Again, doubling, role reversal and soliloquy were used.

4.9 USING NEWSPAPERS

A workshop was advertised as a sociodramatic exploration of the news. The story chosen was to do with the political and economic changes in Russia. A scene was created in which all the economic actors – from a Western banker to a peasant farmer – existed. The subsequent action showed what the likely implications were of economic change and which roles held what power.

4.10 COMMUNITY DEVELOPMENT

Sociodrama was used to create the different family structures and the cultural, racial and ethnic mix of a typical housing estate so that community activists could explore what the basis was for establishing links between people on the estate. One example of a possible link was between older people living on their own and young single parents without any local family ties. The link was called 'fostering grandparents'. By enacting this scene it was then found necessary to add in the professionals who worked in the area, as the link would need to go through them if the connections were to be made. Similarly, community buildings needed to be added (identified by chairs) to the link chain as the connections needed to have a neutral venue as a meeting place.

4.11 COMMUNITY CHANGE

A day workshop was run, using Boal's forum theatre as a base, looking at an inner-city community, with typical issues of poverty, poor housing, race and crime. During the day a group of 20 people developed three themes:

- confrontation with a housing official
- tackling environmental pollution
- dealing with vagrants.

These themes were arrived at by placing large sheets of paper on the floor, on which the group brainstormed all the issues which were then collated into the three themes. In the evening, a further 70 people joined in. Each of the scenes was run through once and then a second time, when the audience was invited to join in, to explore alternative ways of tackling the problems.

In a further workshop in a neighbouring community, housing issues were explored through developing, over a day, a series of scenes following the plight of a tenant in attempting to get their front door repaired. This enabled the group to look at the issue from a number of different perspectives – workperson, councillor, housing manager etc. – as well as trying out alternative strategies. Other themes that emerged were domestic violence and the national political agenda.

4.12 GENDER

Working with a predominantly female group, a woman's body was built on the floor, with participants taking the roles of different parts of the body. A dialogue then ensued between the various roles, for example, between the sexual organs, the heart and the brain, exploring aspects of the female gender role.

Use was made of role reversal and 'voices' from 'off stage' who became the societal forces (for example, parents, church) which influenced the development of the role.

4.13 EXPLORING DIFFERENCES

At a conference in Jerusalem, a sociodrama workshop was advertised on the theme 'We are different – so what?'. From the warm-up the theme that emerged was the cultural and religious differences between Jews and Catholics. This was developed sociodramatically by following the marriage between a prosperous Jewish girl and a poor Catholic boy, the birth of their child, their fleeing from Israel to Argentina and their eventual return to Israel.

The various roles that were created included parent, priest, rabbi, grandparent, child and family friend. The themes explored were cultural and religious differences, dealing with family conflict, the role of families, loss, separation and change.

Bibliography

REFERENCES

Boal, A. (1992) *Games for Actors and Non-actors*. London: Routledge.

Boal, A. (1995) *The Rainbow of Desire*. London: Routledge.

Clayton, M. (1993) *Living Pictures of the Self: Applications of Role Theory in Professional Practice and Daily Living*. Australia: ICA Press.

Kellerman, P. (1996) 'Sociodrama: a group-as-a-whole method for social exploration.' University of Jerusalem, unpublished paper.

McMillan, I. and Wiener, R. (1988) 'Preparing the caretakers for placement.' *Adoption and Fostering 12*, 1, 20–22.

Moreno, J. (1993) *Who shall Survive?* McLean, VA: American Society of Group Psychotherapy and Psychodrama.

Wiener, R. and Traynor, J. (1987–88) 'The use of sociodrama in staff training in working with older people.' *Practice 1*, 4, 332–338.

FURTHER READING

Fitzduff, M. (1988) *Community Conflict Skills*. N. Ireland: Community Conflict Skills Project.

Fox, J. (ed) (1987) *The Essential Moreno*. New York: Springer Publishing Company.

Holmes, P. and Karp, M. (eds) (1991) *Psychodrama: Inspiration and Technique*. London: Routledge.

Holmes, P., Karp, M. and Watson, T. (eds) (1994) *Psychodrama since Moreno*. London: Routledge.

Sternberg, P. and Garcia, A. (1989) *Sociodrama: Who's in Your Shoes?* New York: Praeger.

Subject
Index

Author
Index